67 cooks from **Wales, Ireland, Scotland,**
Isle of Man and **Cornwall** tell you about
traditional and contemporary Celtic cuisine.
By **Gilli Davies.**

Celtic
cuisine

GRAFFEG

Published by Graffeg
First published 2008
Copyright © Graffeg 2008
ISBN 9781905582105

Celtic Cuisine.
Written by Gilli Davies.
Researched by Manisha Harkins.

Graffeg,
Radnor Court,
256 Cowbridge Road East,
Cardiff CF5 1GZ Wales UK.
Tel: +44 (0)29 2037 7312
sales@graffeg.com
www.graffeg.com

Graffeg are hereby identified
as the authors of this work in
accordance with section 77 of the
Copyrights, Designs and Patents
Act 1988.

Distributed by the Welsh Books
Council www.cllc.org.uk
castellbrychan@cllc.org.uk

A CIP Catalogue record for this
book is available from the British
Library.

Designed and produced by
Peter Gill & Associates
sales@petergill.com
www.petergill.com

The publishers are also grateful
to the Welsh Books Council
for their financial support and
marketing advice.
www.gwales.com

Every effort has been made to
ensure that the information in this
book is current and it is given
in good faith at the time of
publication. Please be aware that
circumstances can change and
be sure to check details before
visiting any of the restaurants
featured.

Picture credits:
© aber / Alamy: 51, © Apex News and
Pictures Agency / Alamy: 8,
© britainonview/ Dennis Barnes: 11,
© britainonview/ Duncan Davis: 8,
© britainonview/ Richard Watson: 10,
© Crown Copyright: 14, 17, 19, 49, 92, 130,
145, © Foodanddrinkphotos.com: 14, 36, 40,
66, 81, 112, 133, 136, © Harry Williams: 69,
© Holmes Garden Photos / Alamy: 9,
© Kiran Ridley: 62, © Mark ZYLBER / Alamy:
11, © Peter Gill & Associates: 17, 71,
© Photolibrary Group: 3, 7, 13, 32, 83, 103,
109, 165, 172, © StockFood.com / Banderob,
Heino: 153, © StockFood.com / Bischof,
Harry: 12, 44, © StockFood.com / Carlson,
Tate: 149, © StockFood.com / Caste, Alain: 14,
135, © StockFood.com / Cazals, Jean: 15, 159,
© StockFood.com / Cimbal, Walter: 29,
© StockFood.com / DeSanto, Thom: 162,
© StockFood.com / Drool Ltd, William
Lingwood: 73, © StockFood.com / Eising: 78,
107, 117, © StockFood.com / Ellert, L: 129,
© StockFood.com / Fisher, Tara: 57,
© StockFood.com / Foodcollection: 87,
© StockFood.com / Hamon, J.-F: 180,
© StockFood.com / Heinze, Winfried: 89, 120,
© StockFood.com / Hrbková, Alena: 15, 146,
© StockFood.com / Jackson, James: 179,
© StockFood.com / King, Dave: 154,
© StockFood.com / Krieg, Roland: 76,
© StockFood.com / Lehmann, Joerg: 17, 138,
© StockFood.com / Leser, Nicolas: 3, 12, 20,
126, © StockFood.com / Marsh Alan: 91,
© StockFood.com / Mauduech/Lebain: 35,
© StockFood.com / Maximilian Stock Ltd: 185,
© StockFood.com / Morris Robert: 16,
© StockFood.com / Rynio: 52 © StockFood.
com / Schliack, Amos: 122, © StockFood.com
/ Shooter, Howard: 141, © StockFood.com /
Studio Adna: 12, 15, 24, 175, © StockFood.
com / Strauß, F: 171, © StockFood.com /
Teubner Foodfoto: 96

Celtic
cuisine

Dedication

I would like to dedicate this book to all the cooks and professional chefs who gave their time and recipes in its preparation. And also to Manisha Harkins who provided the initial research. It has been a great pleasure to work with them all. Gilli Davies

GRAFFEG

starters - soups and stews - Fish - Game and poultry - Puddings

Introduction

Gathering recipes for this Celtic cookery book has been a stimulating experience highlighting a common thread of cookery skills, ingredients and culinary traditions throughout the Celtic countries. Perhaps the most rewarding aspect though, has been the enthusiasm and pride in local recipes shown by the cooks and chefs who have contributed from France, Wales, Cornwall, Ireland, Scotland and the Isle of Man.

The ingredients of the Celtic regions are some of the finest possible. With excellent and unspoilt coastlines, the fish, shellfish and sea vegetables are plentiful. Inland, the rivers sport good fish too, and the Celts being good stockmen have always bred the finest breeds of cattle, pigs and sheep. Wild deer and other game are still available and the hedgerows, moors and open spaces harbour a myriad of exciting, untamed ingredients to add flavour such as berries, blossoms, fungi and herbs.

The Celts have deep roots in European history and can be traced back over 25 centuries to 500BC. They have been one of the greatest peoples and were established across a vast area from Britain and Ireland in the north to Spain and France in the south, and spreading east to southern Germany, the Alps, Bohemia and later Italy, the Balkans and even central Turkey. First identified in Switzerland and known as the Celts of La Tène, history shows how the Celtic speakers shared many common bonds of language, customs, art and culture. Known in France as Gauls and Galatae to the Greeks, it was the Romans with their conquering armies who drove the Celts north from Italy and Spain, then later southern France.

and shellfish - Vegetarian - Meat - Baking - Drinks and preserves

By the end of the first century only the British Isles were left and when the Roman Emperor Claudius invaded Britain in AD43 his troops worked their way up to the highlands of Scotland, known as Caledonia. Ireland was the only part of the Celtic world to escape Rome. Later, in the sixth century a resurgence in Celtic culture took western Britons across the channel to establish Brittany.

The Celtic revival of the early Middle Ages was halted by the Vikings and subsequent centuries saw a weakening of the Celts' identity as Wales lost her independence and Brittany was subsumed within France. Scotland was unified with England during the reign of Elizabeth I and Ireland was incorporated into the United Kingdom in 1801. Over the past two centuries the Celtic parts of the British Isles have struggled with their culture and language. However, with the emergence of vigorous nationalist movements, today Celtic tongues are spoken in most of the regions and a sense of shared culture has developed within art, music and of course, cooking.

Traditionally the Celts cooked over an open fire. A large pot would be suspended over the glowing coals and stews and soups were produced. This is not a style of cooking that suits us today, however the griddle, a cookery implement that has stood the test of time, is still very much used in many of the Celtic regions. At one time bread was baked slowly on the griddle by the Celts, but today it is used mainly for cooking a variety of pancakes. In Brittany these are still the thin crisp crêpes, but in Ireland you might well find potato cakes, oatcakes in Scotland and Welsh cakes in Wales, and it is of interest to see how the regional variations have developed.

Oats were once the staple of all the regions but today buckwheat is favoured in Brittany in pancakes, while potatoes major in Ireland and wheat is the most common grain used in Wales. Regional variations in the names of ingredients change too as with the spring onion, which is known as a scallion in Ireland, gibbons in Wales and syboes in Scotland.

Cookery does not stand still though and recipes develop with every generation of cook in the kitchen. This cookbook therefore covers a range of recipes from the traditional dishes rooted in Celtic past, with modern interpretations of old fashioned recipes and some that are at the forefront of modern cooking. As an example of how the old can be mixed successfully with the new, and ingredients transported from one region to another, here is a menu of a breakfast that you might well have enjoyed while visiting Colin and Jacquie Rouse at their Allt Y Golau Farmhouse in Felingwm Uchaf, Carmarthenshire in Wales.

Fruit juices (including homemade lemonade)
Grapefruit, fruit compote, fresh melon, organic yogurt,
Selection of fruit and cereals.

Locally made sausages, Carmarthen bacon, homegrown free range eggs,
 wild mushrooms and tomatoes
Omelette with freshly cut herbs
Bacon and cheese butty
Welsh cheese on toast
Manx kippers with butter

Croissants
Bara Gwenith (home made bread)
Rolls and muffins
Selection of home made preserves
Cafetière coffee and Welsh tea.

Oats were once the staple of all the regions but today buckwheat is favoured in Brittany in pancakes, while potatoes major in Ireland and wheat is the most common grain used in Wales.

67 cooks from **Wales, Ireland, Scotland, Brittany, Isle of Man** and **Cornwall** tell you about their traditional and contemporary Celtic cuisine.

Darina Allen
Ballymaloe Cookery School, Ireland: 21, 93.

Sheila Allen
Fanny's Café, Wales: 74.

Mrs Ann Barney
Yethen Isaf, Wales: 46.

Nick Bevan
Chelsea Café, Swansea, Wales: 59.

Vijay Bhagotra
Celtic Cauldron, Wales: 31.

Wendy Brandon
Wendy Brandon's Handmade Preserves, Wales: 173, 182.

Catherine Brown
Author of 'Broths to Bannocks', Scotland: 79, 157.

Georgina Campbell
Food writer, Ireland: 33, 116, 119, 128, 147.

Colin Clydesdale
Stravaigin, Glasgow, Scotland: 26, 115.

Ronnie Clydesdale
The Ubiquitous Chip, Scotland: 30, 38, 158.

Emily Cosgrove
High Tide Café, Swansea, Wales: 45, 80.

Colin Craig and Lesley Crosfield
The Albannach, Lochinver, Scotland: 22, 166.

Alan Craigie
The Creel Inn Restaurant with Rooms, Scotland: 23.

Pat Cross
Whitehouse Guest House, Penycwm, Wales: 25, 28, 100.

Recipes are attributed to the people and places where they were first discovered.

Jackie Dare
Cynyll Farm, Llangadog, Wales: 79, 85.

Beatrix Davies
The Manor House Hotel, Wales: 27.

Ben Davies
Llangoed Hall, Llyswen, Wales: 68.

Gilli Davies
Food writer, Wales: 33, 42, 53, 75, 77, 99, 102, 104, 110, 137, 144, 148, 155.

Paul Davies
Fairyhill, Reynoldston, Wales: 21, 31.

Sue Farmer
The Bay Tree, Holywood, Ireland: 72.

Theodora Fitzgibbon
Author of 'The Art of British Cooking', Scotland: 61, 114, 181, 183.

Gerry Galvin
Drimcong House Restaurant, Ireland: 98, 127, 161, 176, 183, 184.

Marie Galvin
Drimcong House, County Galway, Ireland: 164.

Birdie Gardiner
Mohober, Mullinahone, Ireland: 90.

Jayne George
Farthings Wine Bar, Cowbridge, Wales: 84.

Mary Gilbert
The Crinan Hotel, Argyll, Scotland: 139, 168.

Mary Ann Gilchrist
Carlton Riverside, Wales: 54, 101.

Ken Goody
Cemlyn Restaurant, Wales: 151.

Joyce Hart
Glasfryn Guest House and Restaurant, Brechfa, Wales: 147.

Eamon Harty
Mor Chluana Restaurant, Ireland: 45, 121, 178.

Jane Heard
Tregynon Country Farmhouse Hotel, Wales: 142.

Non Henderson
Country cook, Wales: 186.

Margaret Horn
But 'N Ben, Auchmithie, Scotland: 95, 97, 100.

Recipes are attributed to the people and places where they were first discovered.

Recipes are attributed to the people and places where they were first discovered.

Michael Smith
Author of 'A Cook's Tour of Britain': 56, 157.

Rick Stein
The Seafood Restaurant, Padstow, Cornwall: 67.

Meudwen Stephens
Country cook, Wales:158.

Sonia Stevenson
The Old Chapel, Bethany, Cornwall: 187.

Jenny Thomson
The Butterchurn, Fife, Scotland: 41, 134, 155, 169, 187.

S. Minwel Tibbott
Author of 'Welsh Fare', Wales: 163, 182.

Kevin Viner
Viner's Restaurant and Bar, Cornwall: 55.

Martin and Clare Vowell
Tir a Mor Restaurant, Criccieth, Wales: 53, 61.

Janet Warren
Author of 'A Feast of Scotland', Scotland: 47, 48, 54, 118.

Allison Whowell
Goetre Isaf, Bangor, Wales: 74, 85, 123, 143.

David Wilson
The Peat Inn, Fife, Scotland: 43.

Craig Wood
Crinan Hotel, Argyll, Scotland: 64, 124.

Recipes are attributed to the people and places where they were first discovered.

Recipes list

Vegetarian

Meat

Game and poultry

Puddings

metric and imperial measures

Conversion tables

One American cup equivalent in metric and imperial (British) ounces. Here are some basic ingredients listed in American cups with their equivalents in metric and imperial measures.

One American cup	Metric grams	Imperial ounces
butter	225g	8oz
flour	100g	4oz
sugar	200g	7oz
currants	150g	5oz
cooking apples, peeled and sliced	100g	4oz
beans, dried	175g	6oz
breadcrumbs, fresh	140g	4½oz
currants, dried	150g	5oz
flour, plain and self raising	175g	6oz
honey, syrup or jam	350g	12oz
mushrooms, sliced	50g	2oz
nuts, whole almonds and hazelnuts	150g	5oz
oats, rolled	75g	3oz
potatoes, cooked and mashed	225g	8oz
long grain rice, uncooked	200g	7oz
strawberries, fresh hold	150g	5oz
sugar, granulated or caster	200g	7oz
tomatoes, canned in juice	225g	8oz
tomatoes, fresh, quartered	150g	5oz
milk or cream	225ml	8fl oz
oil	225ml	8fl oz

starters,
and

In the past, juices or soups surrounding the one pot casserole made up the first course, however throughout Celtic countries the coastline has provided the simplest starters of all.

Fresh Dublin Bay prawns, Scottish scallops, Breton moules and Welsh cockles. There are a number of traditional dishes such as potted fish or meat, and fish and game terrines. Meat or vegetable tartlets or flavourful game sausages can also make for a tasty starter.

You will find a selection of such dishes in this chapter, from Irish venison sausages and Manx potted herring to tasty deep fried Welsh cockles or to a delectable Scots game terrine filled with local delicacies. Try them all for an apt introduction to the glories of the Celtic table.

first courses
light dishes

Raking cockles by hand at Penclawdd, designated a sustainable fishery by the Marine Stewardship Council.

warm salad with
crispy cockles,
laver and bacon

Deep fried Penclawdd cockles

Paul Davies, Fairyhill, Reynoldston, Wales. For this recipe, use your deep fat fryer and wire basket. These crispy cockles could be used in a number of different ways e.g. a warm salad with crispy cockles, laver and bacon or as part of a seafood platter.

Ingredients

225g (8oz) cooked shelled
  cockles
flour for coating
salt and pepper

1 Rinse the cockles in cold water then squeeze gently to drain.
2 Toss in seasoned flour and shake to remove the excess.
3 Preheat fryer to 190°C, 375°F.
4 Carefully tip the floured cockles into the fryer. Cook for approximately 4 to 5 minutes. The cockles should be crispy and not chewy.

5 Drain the cockles on absorbent paper. Add salt and pepper to taste.
6 Serve as an interesting canapé.

Chicken and bacon press

Darina Allen, Ballymaloe Cookery School, Ireland. This recipe was handed down through mother-in-law Myrtle Allen's family and is still in frequent use. Originally it was a handy way of using up a boiling fowl past its prime, but nowadays it is almost impossible to find a boiling fowl, either before or after its prime!

Ingredients

1 large 2-3kg (4-6lb) boiling fowl
900g (2lb) lean streaky bacon in
  one piece
2 onions
2 carrots
1 stalk celery
a few parsley stalks
a few sprigs of thyme and maybe
  a sprig of marjoram
5 peppercorns
2 tablespoons chopped parsley

Serves 6-8

1 Put the boiling fowl and bacon into a saucepan with the onions, carrot, celery, herbs, salt and a few peppercorns.
2 Add about 5cm (2in) of water. Bring to the boil, cover and cook in a moderate oven (180°C, 350°F, gas mark 4) for 1½ to 2 hours, depending on the size and age of the chicken. Discard the vegetables.
3 When the chicken and bacon are cooked, skin and chop the meat into 2cm (¾in) dice while it is still hot. Add the parsley, taste and correct the seasoning, then press into a bowl.

4 Pour a little of the cooking liquid over the top, cover with a plate and weight it down. Leave the mixture overnight in the fridge.
5 Cut into slices and serve with a salad.
6 A more elaborate version can be made by layering the chicken, bacon and chopped parsley.

Game terrine of wild boar, pheasant
breast, mountain hare and guinea fowl with a rowan berry sauce

Colin Craig and Lesley Crosfield, The Albannach, Lochinver, Scotland. Standing in a small glen overlooking the Albannach is a 19th century house with plenty of character. This recipe exploits the bountiful game available on their doorstep.

Ingredients

For the terrine

225g (8oz) wild boar sausages (or good pork will do), skins removed

325g (12oz) mix of skinned pheasant breast, hare saddle, and guinea fowl breast (or other available mixed game), diced but not too finely

sufficient good quality back bacon to line a 500g (1lb) loaf tin, flattened with a rolling pin or the back of a large knife

For the marinade

2 tablespoons good quality olive oil

1 large onion, finely chopped

2 garlic cloves, finely chopped

finely grated rind of 1 lemon

plenty of black pepper and good pinch of sea salt

2 large sprigs of fresh thyme, stalks removed (sage or rosemary can be substituted)

100ml (4fl oz) port wine

For the rowan sauce

grated rind and juice of ½ lemon and ½ orange

100g (4oz) of good rowan jelly (red currant can be substituted)

½ leaf of gelatine, soaked in water then squeezed out

approx. 100ml (4fl oz) port wine

1 teaspoon Dijon mustard

Serves 6-8

For the salad

Mixed leaves available; rocket is good but any interesting leaves will do

a little olive oil and vinegar to dress

a few red currants to garnish

1 To make the marinade: heat a large, heavy bottomed pan with the olive oil. Add the onion and garlic. Sauté gently until opaque, without browning.

2 Add the lemon rind, pepper and thyme, stir briefly then add the port. Cook on medium heat, stirring regularly, until the mixture resembles moist marmalade. Remove from the stove and allow to cool.

3 Meanwhile prepare the terrine. Mix sausage meat and game thoroughly with the cooled marinade in a large glass bowl and allow to stand overnight in a cool place.

4 Line a 500g (1lb) loaf tin with baking foil. Line the bottom and sides of the tin with the flattened bacon leaving surplus hanging over the edge for covering the terrine mixture. Tip the game mixture in the tin, pressing with your fingers to fill evenly.

5 Bring the ends of the bacon up to cover the mixture, using trimmings to fill gaps. Cover the tin with another piece of foil, then place in a roasting tray filled with

sufficient boiling water to come two-thirds of the way up the side of the tin.

6 Place in the middle of a preheated oven – 180°C, 350°F, gas mark 4 and cook for about 1 hour and 15 minutes.

7 Remove from the oven, press terrine using a second loaf tin weighted with a tin of beans or similar. Allow to cool for about 2 hours. Refrigerate for several more hours or even overnight if possible.

8 Make the sauce: put all the ingredients together in a small heavy bottomed pan and heat gently until the jelly has melted, stirring regularly. Allow to cool, then refrigerate for several hours.

9 To serve: arrange slices of the terrine about 2cm (¾in) thick, on plates. Pile some mixed salad leaves alongside (not too fussily) Dress with a little olive oil and vinegar, then carefully spoon a little of the rowan sauce beside the terrine, garnish with the red currants.

Orcadian salt cod terrine

Alan Craigie, The Creel Inn Restaurant with Rooms, Orkney, Scotland. This is an Orkney version of a French brandade, incorporating a strong local flavour – salt cod.

Ingredients

450g (1lb) salt cod (soaked for 24 hours in fresh, cold water, changing water 2 – 3 times)
2 cloves garlic, chopped
1 medium onion chopped
100ml (4fl oz) olive oil
50ml (2fl oz) double cream
large pinch of freshly chopped parsley

Serves 4

1 Poach the salt cod in fresh water for 7 minutes.
2 Cook the garlic and onion gently in the olive oil until soft but not brown.
3 Transfer to a food processor and blend until smooth. Add the cooked salt cod and pulse until smooth.
4 Bring the cream to a simmer and blend it in the mixture by hand. Add the freshly chopped parsley.

5 Dampen some cling film with cold water. Line the terrine dish with the cling film using kitchen paper to push the cling film into the corners of the dish. Add the creamy fish mixture, place in the fridge and chill.
6 To remove the brandade pull gently on the cling film and the brandade will slide out of the terrine dish.
7 Slice the brandade to serve. It can be accompanied by hot toast and dressed salad leaves.

salt cod

accompanied by hot toast
and dressed salad leaves

Fresh salmon
toss with sea salt and sugar

Fresh salmon salt-cured with dill

Kathleen O'Sullivan, Sea View House Hotel and Restaurant, Ballylikey, Ireland.
Glengarriff's sheltered position on Bantry Bay, surrounded as it is with a ring of mountains, provides the gentlest of climates where subtropical plants thrive. Just offshore is Garnish Island, which is covered in a variety of subtropical vegetation. Fishermen nearby will be glad to take you across to the island.

Ingredients

900g (2lb) fresh salmon, centre cut in one piece, skin and bones removed
4 tablespoons white peppercorns
4 tablespoons black peppercorns
4 tablespoons sea salt
4 tablespoons sugar
3 bunches of fresh dill

Serves 8

1 Wash the salmon inside out and pat dry with kitchen towel.
2 Using a blender, or spice grinder, coarsely grind the peppercorns and toss with sea salt and sugar. Rub this mixture all over the salmon, inside and out. It is important to use up the entire amount, so press it into the salmon with the flat of your hand if necessary. Spread a third of the dill in the bottom of a non-metallic dish that will hold the salmon in one piece.
3 Put the salmon on top of the dill, and tuck a third of the dill inside of the salmon. Scatter the rest of the dill over the top.
4 Cover the salmon, not the dish, with cling film and weight it with a plate slightly smaller than the circumference of the dish. Place a heavy object on the plate – such as a large can of tomatoes or a foil wrapped brick.
5 Refrigerate for 5 days, turning once a day and replacing weight. Juices will accumulate in the bottom of the dish. Leave these as they help to marinate the fish.
6 Scrape all the spices and dill off the salmon and return to the refrigerator until ready to serve.
7 Thinly slice the salmon and serve chilled with lemon wedges and tiny capers, or whisk together some prepared mustard, minced dill, lemon juice, and a little oil to make a sauce.

Laverbread and bacon pots

Pat Cross, Whitehouse, Penycwm, Wales. The seaweed, laverbread, is traditionally served with bacon and this recipe also uses another local flavour, Llangloffan cheese.

Ingredients

200g (7oz) streaky smoked bacon cut into lardons
black pepper
200g (7oz) laverbread
2 tablespoons lemon juice
4 tablespoons double cream
200g (7oz) Llangloffan cheese, grated (or any strong cheddar cheese)

Serves 4

1 Dry fry the bacon in a non-stick pan until crisp, add the laverbread.
2 Continue cooking for 1 to 2 minutes. Season with black pepper and add the lemon juice.
3 Divide between 4 grill proof serving dishes or ramekins. Pour 1 tablespoon of cream over each and sprinkle the cheese evenly.
4 Put under a hot grill until golden and bubbling.
5 Serve with crusty fresh bread.

stacked thyme and sage tattie scones

with wild mushrooms

Colin Clydesdale, Stravaigin, Glasgow, Scotland. Scotland, at the right time of the year, has an abundance of wild mushrooms, making this dish an easy and obvious vegetarian dish. If you can't source wild mushrooms then that strange anomaly 'the farmed wild mushroom' will do!

Ingredients

For the duxelle

450g (1lb) wild mushrooms cleaned thoroughly and chopped finely
2 cloves garlic, crushed
1 medium onion, finely chopped
2 teaspoons olive oil
25g (1oz) butter
1 tablespoon sherry
2 sticks celery, finely chopped
1 tablespoon double cream
salt and pepper
1 small sprig fresh tarragon, finely chopped

For the tattie scones

225g (8oz) potatoes, peeled, boiled and mashed
1 sprig each fresh thyme, sage, rosemary, finely chopped
450g (1lb) plain flour
salt and pepper

Serves 4

1 To make the duxelle: in a large thick bottomed pot, sauté the garlic and onion in the oil and butter until a little brown. Then add the chopped mushrooms. Sauté gently for a few minutes before adding the sherry, celery, cream, seasoning and fresh tarragon.

2 Allow the whole mix to simmer gently for about 10 minutes, stirring constantly to avoid sticking.

3 To make the scones: in the largest mixing bowl you possess, combine the potato, herbs and half the flour. (This is a very messy job, often resulting in the cook getting covered in bits of tattie scone). Combine until all the flour has been incorporated. If the mix is still a little gluey, add a little more flour until it has dried out, don't be alarmed if the amount of flour seems very large, this is often the case.

4 Season to taste, then roll out on a floured board to 4mm (¼in) thick.

5 Cut into small rounds before gently frying in a lightly buttered frying pan. They take about 2 minutes either side.

6 To build the dish, lay a tattie scone in the middle of the plate and top with a spoonful of duxelle. Repeat the whole process until the tower is about 4 tattie scones high.

Note: If you have an excess of wild mushrooms, try sauteing a few whole mushrooms in a little oil, then deglaze them with some blue cheese and balsamic vinegar. These make a great foil to the slightly creamy duxelle. Garnish the whole lot with toasted pumpkin seeds and if you're feeling extravagant, some deep fried shallot crisps.

Tiny batter cakes of Penclawdd cockles and laverbread on a bed on wilted leaves, with wild garlic mayonnaise or steamed Cleddau mussels

Beatrix Davies, formerly of The Manor House Hotel, Fishguard, Wales. The hotel is perched high above Fishguard Harbour from where Beatrix would source much of her seafood.

Ingredients

75g (3oz) cooked cockles
100g (4oz) plain flour
just under 300ml (½pt) milk
 so that batter isn't overly wet
1 egg
1 egg white, beaten until fairly
 stiff
2 dessertspoons of laverbread
 or to taste
salt and pepper to taste
oil

To Serve

Either: mixed salad, lemon juice,
 butter, wild garlic, good
 quality mayonnaise
Or: mussels, light vinaigrette

Makes 16 cakes

1 Make a pancake batter using the flour, milk and egg and allow to stand for about 20 minutes. Then fold in the beaten egg white.

2 Add the laverbread and seasoning, and mix well. Add cockles to your liking – not too many or the mixture will fall apart when cooked.

3 In a large frying pan, heat a little oil (just enough to coat the base with a thick film) until very hot. Add small dessertspoons of the batter mixture, flip over and cook the other side.

4 Serve immediately on a bed of mixed salad leaves briefly sautéed in butter and lemon juice. Chop some wild garlic into the mayonnaise, mix and place a small helping with a spot of lemon juice on the plate.

5 Alternatively, if you want to impress, steam some succulent Cleddau mussels, take out of their shells and serve with a light vinaigrette as a contrast to the cockle cakes.

Manx potted herring

Traditional, Isle of Man. This is not a typical 'potted' dish like potted crab (which uses clarified butter to preserve the meat or fish) but a dish traditionally cooked in a large pot or earthenware casserole.

Ingredients

6 fresh herrings
1 tablespoon pickling spice
vinegar and water in equal
    proportions
1 or 2 bay leaves
seasoning

Serves 6

1 Take the heads and tails off the herrings, and clean thoroughly.
2 Bone and roll each one up, skin side out. Place them alongside one another in an ovenproof dish.
3 Sprinkle with pickling spice. Cover with vinegar and water and add the bay leaves and seasoning.
4 Cover with a tightly fitting lid or foil.
5 Bake at 150ºC, 300°F, gas mark 2 for 1 to 1½ hours. Serve hot or cold.

Fried Welsh goats cheese with rhubarb and ginger sauce

Pat Cross, Whitehouse, Penycwm, Wales. This looks very pretty if young pink rhubarb is used for the sauce. It can be picked in season and frozen in ice cube trays for use throughout the year. (Plain soft goats cheese can be sliced and then rolled in fresh breadcrumbs if the chevelles are difficult to find).

Ingredients

1 pk x 125g (5oz) Pant ys Gawn
    goats cheese chevelles
    (coated with breadcrumbs)
sunflower oil
1l (1¾pt) rhubarb and ginger
    sauce (as below)
mixed salad leaves to serve

For the rhubarb and ginger sauce

450g (1lb) new season pink
    rhubarb
2.5cm (1in) fresh ginger, finely
    grated
2 tablespoons caster sugar
2 tablespoons water

Serves 2

1 To make the rhubarb and ginger sauce: put all of the ingredients into a small pan and cover with a lid. Slowly heat and simmer until the rhubarb is soft and beginning to break up.
2 Either puree in a blender or use a blending stick until very smooth. Leave to cool, and if not using immediately, then put into ice cube trays and freeze. Use one cube per person – defrost for serving.
3 Fry the cheese in a little sunflower oil until crisp and golden. Leave to cool. Arrange mixed leaves on serving plates with the cheese and a pool of sauce to the side.

Manx potted herring

Sprinkle with pickling spice
bay leaves and seasoning

Marinated smoked finnan haddie

with quail egg

Ronnie Clydesdale, The Ubiquitous Chip, Glasgow, Scotland. The Ubiquitous Chip opened in January 1971 with the firm idea of bringing Scotland's endangered cuisine out of the home and into the restaurant: even to assert that Scotland had a cuisine and some of the finest raw materials anywhere. Note: Syboes are the Irish scallions, the Welsh gibbons or the English spring onions.

Ingredients

500g (1lb 2oz) peat or oak smoked finnan haddie fillets
olive oil
450g (1lb) new turnips or swede, peeled and cut into matchsticks
6 fronds fresh dill, chopped
6 radishes
6 syboes, 2.5cm (1in) of bulb only
6 quails eggs
6 slices of lemon
6 fronds of fresh dill

Serves 6

1 Slice the haddies finely – be meticulous about removing the bones – and place in a stainless or glazed bowl. Pour in the lemon juice, mix well and leave for 20 minutes

2 Add the olive oil. Peel the turnips and cut into matchsticks and add to the bowl with the chopped dill. Mix well.

3 Top the radishes and syboes and cut flower-like incisions at the top. Place in iced water.

4 Poach the quails eggs until 'mollet' – firm but still slightly soft inside – about 2 minutes in boiling water. Cool the eggs immediately under cold water. Shell.

5 Arrange the haddie mixture on 6 starter plates, decorate with a lemon slice, a radish flower, a syboe flower and the poached quails egg topped with a dill frond. Accompany with good wholemeal bread or toast.

Conger eel cooked in butter

Simone Morand, 'Cuisine Traditionnelle De Bretagne'. Choose the piece near the head, the tail being full of bones. Keep the latter for soup or stock.

Ingredients

6 slices x 2cm (1in) thickness conger eel
150ml (¼pt) milk
3 tablespoons seasoned flour
25g (1oz) butter
1 tablespoon oil
pepper
lemon
chopped parsley

Serves 6

1 Soak the conger eel slices in the milk for ½ hour.

2 Drain and dry on kitchen roll, then toss each slice in the flour.

3 Heat the butter and oil in the pan gently without letting it brown.

4 Fry the conger eel on each side until golden brown.

5 Cook slowly for 10 minutes, add pepper and serve with the lemon and parsley.

Laverbread and oatmeal slices

Vijay Bhagotra, formerly of Celtic Cauldron, Cardiff, Wales. Here's an easy recipe combining three classic Welsh ingredients: laverbread, oatmeal and bacon. With the bacon fat added, the result is a starter with a truly local flavour. Vegetarians can substitute bacon fat for vegetable oil.

Ingredients

225g (8oz) laverbread
125g (5oz) oatmeal
3 tablespoons vegetable oil or
    bacon fat
garnish with snipped rashers of
    bacon and a slice of lemon

Serves 4

1 Mix the laverbread with the oatmeal so that it makes a firm mixture. Divide into 4 parts and roll into balls.
2 Heat the vegetable oil or bacon fat in a shallow frying pan. Put each ball in one at a time.
3 While cooking for half a minute, press down until the pancake becomes thin. Turn 2-3 times until nice and crispy on both sides.

4 Serve on a slice of buttered toast with snippets of bacon and a slice of lemon.

Scrambled eggs with cockles and roasted peppers served on a garlic crouton

Paul Davies, Fairyhill, Reynoldston, Gower, Wales. This dish was inspired by the Provençale dish of piperade. It is versatile as you could add different seafood, or for vegetarians perhaps some nuts or seeds.

Ingredients

8 eggs
1 red and 1 yellow pepper,
    roasted and cut in strips
4 slices bread
2 cloves garlic, halved
olive oil
150ml (5fl oz) double cream
salt and freshly ground black
    pepper
100g (4oz) fresh cockles
chopped chives

Serves 4

1 For the roasted peppers: place peppers in a hot oven until brown and blistered. Remove and put in a plastic bag to cool. When cool, split in half, remove seeds and skin. Cut into 5mm strips. Put to one side.
2 Cut 3 heart-shaped croutons from each slice of bread. Rub with cut garlic and fry in some olive oil until golden and crisp. Drain well and keep warm.
3 Whisk the eggs and cream together with some salt and black pepper.

4 Place a little olive oil in a pan and add most of the peppers (reserve 4 red and 4 yellow strips for garnish). Add the egg mixture and start to scramble. When half scrambled add the cockles and continue to cook until desired consistency is achieved.
5 Place three croutons on each plate, arrange scrambled eggs in the middle and place a cross of pepper on top of each portion and sprinkle with chopped chives.

Welsh rarebit Perhaps the most famous of all Welsh recipes

Always a favourite in Wales and in Medieval times

Venison sausages

Georgina Campbell, food writer, Ireland. Home-made sausages are highly appreciated in Ireland and there's hot competition amongst butchers for the annual prizes for the best sausages and black and white puddings. Venison sausages have excellent flavour and they are easy to make. This recipe suggests hand-shaping the sausages, leaving the tricky business of filling sausage skins well alone.

Ingredients

900g (2lb) finely minced
   venison
450g (1lb) finely minced belly of
   pork
1 level tablespoon salt
1 dessertspoon freshly ground
   pepper
1 clove garlic, crushed
1 teaspoon dried thyme
1 egg, beaten
1 tablespoon flour

Makes 1.4kg (3lb) sausages

1 Combine all the ingredients except the flour in a basin.
2 When thoroughly mixed, roll the sausages to chipolata size with floured hands.
3 Fry in a little oil when required and freeze the remainder.

Welsh rarebit

Gilli Davies, Wales. Perhaps the most famous of all Welsh recipes. Always a favourite in Wales and in Medieval times. Known as 'Roasted Cheese' Welsh rarebit has not always been the rich savoury we now know. It was once a recipe for using tough poor-quality cheese at a time when the cream from the top of the milk was used for butter so only skimmed milk found its way into cheese making.

Ingredients

225g (8oz) grated strong flavoured
   Welsh cheddar cheese
25g (1oz) butter, melted
1 tablespoon Worcester sauce
1 tablespoon mustard
1 tablespoon flour
4 tablespoons beer (brown ale if
   possible)
4 slices bread, toasted on one
   side only
cayenne pepper

Serves 4

1 Grate the cheese and mix with the remaining ingredients, except the bread, to form a firm paste.
2 Spread on the uncooked sides of the four slices of toast and grill gently until the topping is cooked through and well browned.

Soups and

Soups and stew were ideally suited to Celtic cooks. Using the essential cast iron pot with tripod over an open fire, they were cooked simply and slowly.

Like the griddle, the cast iron pot would be fuelled by whatever was available, be it peat, coal, gorse, straw, wood or culm. A good hearty broth with perhaps the addition of the usual staples – either oats, barley or potatoes – and the centrepiece of meat or fish would make a fine meal indeed. Brose was as nourishing as could be in Scotland, cawl in Wales and, of course, Irish stew or brotchan in Ireland.

The ubiquitous onion and later the potato flavoured many varieties of soup or stew, along with root vegetables. In the olden days, it made sense to add a piece of meat kept whole so that it would impart its flavour into the broth. The broth would be served in a bowl while the meat could be kept and served later, as needed – therefore 'eking out' or stretching the resources. The jelly and fat could be reserved for use on the next day for various dishes.

Stews are slow-cooked thicker versions of a hearty soup. In the past, oatmeal dumplings were often added to make the soup or stew even more filling; perhaps seaweed was used in coastal areas for nourishment.

Soups and stews are great for cold winter days and versatile too. Think of some of the most famous Celtic concoctions – Scotch broth, cawl, leek and potato soup, Irish stew – all on the following pages for you to try.

stews

The sharp, acid flavour of sorrel adds a lovely tang to any number of bland dishes and it also makes a superb soup.

twentieth-century recipe

Crab soup

Crab soup

Traditional, Cornwall. Whilst this is very much a twentieth-century recipe it pays excellent homage to an area where crabs were at one time commonplace at the high-tea table.

Ingredients

225g (8oz) crab meat (half dark and half white)
1 large onion, peeled and sliced
1 clove garlic, crushed
1.2l (2pt) fish stock
50g (2oz) butter
25g (1oz) flour
grated rind of 1 orange
300ml (½pt) double cream
1 glass dry sherry
salt and freshly ground white pepper

For the fish stock

900g (2lb) washed sole bones, or any other fish you have to hand
1.2l (2pt) cold water

Serves 4

1 To make the fish stock: cover the sole bones with cold water and bring to a simmer. (There is little gain in ever simmering fish bones for more than 20 to 25 minutes). Drain this stock through a fine sieve or muslin and put aside for use.

2 To make the soup: melt the butter in a heavy bottomed pan. When just foaming, but not coloured, add the onion and garlic. Cover with a lid and soften the onion without colouring.

3 Add the dark crab meat and work in well. Add the flour, stirring in well to avoid lumping. Slowly add the fish stock, stirring all the time until the soup boils. Simmer for 30 minutes.

4 Strain the soup into a clean pan. Season with salt and pepper. Add the cream, sherry and orange rind.

5 Chop the white crab meat and remove any skin or 'blades'. Add the fish to the soup, re-heat and serve immediately.

Cheese soup

Traditional, Ireland. Perhaps a precursor to the more common broccoli and cheese or vegetable and cheese soups of today, this is a simple and tasty way for a dairy rich country to inject some protein into a vegetarian soup.

Ingredients

600ml (1pt) chicken or vegetable stock or water
2 medium onions, peeled and sliced
2 medium potatoes, peeled and sliced
1 carrot, peeled and sliced
2 cloves, tied in muslin
25g (1oz) butter
25g (1oz) flour
150ml (5fl oz) milk
150g (5oz) grated cheddar cheese
salt and pepper
chopped parsley for garnish

Serves 4

1 Bring the stock or water to the boil. Add the vegetables and simmer for 20 minutes along with the cloves.

2 Remove from the heat. Strain the liquid and vegetables through a sieve to make a puree, or liquidise. Set aside.

3 Melt the butter in a saucepan, add the flour and whisk in well.

Add the milk, stirring all the time to avoid lumps.

4 Add the liquid and sieved vegetables. Bring to boil and cook for a few minutes. Lower the heat and stir in the grated cheese together with salt and pepper.

5 Do not boil the soup after the cheese is added as it will curdle.

6 Sprinkle with chopped parsley and serve.

Bacon and cockle chowder

Dafydd Lloyd, Brava Café, Pontcanna, Wales. Chowders are seafood soup-stews thickened with potatoes often added for a smoky flavour. Although they are now commonly associated with New England, their antecedents would have been the fishy soups of the British Isles and cockles and bacon are an ideal combination in this Welsh chowder.

Ingredients

225g (8oz) diced smoked bacon
　or pancetta
350g (12oz) washed cockles
25g (1oz) butter
3 medium potatoes, peeled and
　diced
1 tablespoon flour
2 cleaned leeks, sliced
2 tablespoons parsley, finely
　chopped
750ml (1¼pt) fish stock
pinch of chilli flakes
75ml (3fl oz) double cream
salt and pepper to taste

For the garnish

4 cream crackers
pinch of paprika
1 tablespoon flat leaf parsley

Serves 4

1 Melt the butter and add the bacon. Fry until crisp. Add the diced potatoes and cook for 5 minutes on low heat. Add the flour and stir thoroughly.

2 Add the leeks and parsley, then half of the fish stock. Bring to a simmer stirring, and add the remaining stock and chilli flakes.

3 Simmer for 15 minutes then add the cream and cockles and season to taste. Garnish with cream crackers, paprika and flat leaf parsley.

Cock-a-leekie

Ronnie Clydesdale, The Ubiquitous Chip, Glasgow, Scotland. This peasant dish with many regional variations goes back as far as the 16th century. Some cooks add chopped grilled bacon, some use beef stock, some add Jamaican pepper and many suggest offering stewed prunes with the finished dish. Talleyrand, the French gourmet, recommended cooking prunes in the soup.

Ingredients

1 fresh chicken
12 medium sized leeks, well
　washed and chopped in 2cm
　(¾in) lengths.
100g (4oz) washed rice
3-4 medium sized carrots,
　peeled and grated
salt and crushed black pepper

Serves 4

1 Put the chicken in a pot with enough water to more than cover. Add 6 leeks. Cover the pot and simmer gently for 1 hour or until the chicken is falling off the bone.

2 Remove the chicken and reserve. Strain the stock into a fresh pot, add the rice and cook in a covered pot for 10 minutes.

3 Add the grated carrots and the remainder of the chopped leeks and continue cooking for 20 minutes. Taste for intensity of flavour and, if necessary, reduce further to increase the taste.

4 Season with salt and pepper. Chop a little of the reserved chicken and add to the finished soup.

Note: The reserved chicken is sometimes served as a separate course with mealie or boiled potatoes and a very strong sauce or perhaps yellow mustard.

Bacon and cockle chowder

...add the cream and cockles and season to taste.

Garnish with cream crackers, paprika and flat leaf parsley

cornish broth

one-pot recipe that can be divided into two

stewing beef

onion, cut in half

mixed herbs

2 carrots, peeled and diced

1 parsnip, diced

turnip, diced

flatpoll or other cabbage

salt and pepper

chopped parsley

Cornish broth

Traditional, Cornwall. A typical Celtic one-pot recipe that can be divided into two, meat and vegetables to be eaten separately from the cooking liquid which becomes a nourishing soup.

Ingredients

225g (8oz) stewing beef (in one piece)
1 medium onion, cut in half
a small bunch of mixed herbs
2 carrots, peeled and diced
1 parsnip, diced
100g (4oz) turnip, diced
175g (6oz) flatpoll or other cabbage
salt and pepper
1 tablespoon chopped parsley
2 slices bread, diced into 1cm (½in) cubes

Serves 4

❶ Place the stewing beef (in one piece), onion and bouquet garni in a saucepan and cover with 900ml (1½pt) cold water. Season with 1 teaspoon salt. Bring to the boil and simmer very gently for 1 to 1½ hours.

❷ Add the diced vegetables and continue cooking for 15 minutes. Shred the cabbage and add to the pan, cooking for a further 15 minutes.

❸ Strain the stock into another pan and reduce to 450ml (¾pt).

❹ Slice the meat and keep warm with vegetables. Place the diced bread into bowls and pour the soup over, sprinkle well with milled pepper and parsley.

❺ Serve the meat separately on plates together with the remaining vegetables and a modicum of the soup.

❻ A jacket potato with sour cream or butter would be an ideal accompaniment.

Scotch broth with hodgils (oatmeal dumplings)

Jenny Thomson, formerly of The Butterchurn, Kelty, Fife, Scotland. Jenny says that you can make this broth with or without the hodgils.

Ingredients

1.5l (3pt) lamb stock
75g (3oz) broth mix
1 large carrot, peeled and diced
1 large onion, peeled and diced
1 large leek, washed and sliced
1 small turnip, peeled and diced
1 handful parsley, chopped
salt and pepper

For the hodgils

175g (6oz) medium oatmeal
1 small onion, peeled and chopped
25g (1oz) butter
1 handful of parsley chopped

75g (3oz) beef suet melted and some melted bacon fat if available or substitute with a good cooking oil

Serves 4

❶ To make the broth: put all the ingredients into a pan. Cover with a lid and bring to the boil.

❷ Simmer for about 1 hour or until the peas within the broth mix are soft.

❸ To make the hodgils or dumplings: fry the onion gently in the butter. Add the parsley and the oatmeal. Stir well adding the melted suet and bacon fat a little at a time until you have a soft but firm dough.

❹ Roll the mixture into balls and leave to stand for about 30 minutes.

❺ Cook in the broth for around 15 minutes or roast on a baking sheet in a pre heated oven 200°C, 400°F, gas mark 6 until golden and crisp and use like croutons.

Cawl of bacon with vegetables

'Flavours of Wales' by **Gilli Davies,** published by Gomer Press. This is a traditional recipe that would have been very much a staple in the diet of a Welsh rural family.

Ingredients

1kg (2.2lb) piece of salted bacon or ham, shoulder or corner

1 whole onion

1 whole carrot

1 whole parsnip

1 bay leaf

a bunch of parsley stems and tops used separately

1 large leek, white and green part separated and diced

3 carrots peeled and cubed

2 parsnips peeled and cubed

2 turnips, peeled and cubed

a bunch of fresh winter savoury or sage

salt and pepper

Serves 4-6

1 Soak the bacon or ham overnight in cold water to remove some of the salt.

2 Rinse well and put the piece whole in a large pan with enough cold water to cover. Add the whole onion carrot, parsnip, bay leaf and parsley stalks and simmer gently for an hour then leave to cool and skim the fat from the surface. Remove the bacon from the stock and strain the liquid to keep for later.

3 Slice some of the bacon for a separate meal and cut the remainder into chunks for the cawl.

4 Gently fry the cubed carrots, parsnips, turnips and the bottom white half of the leek in 25g (1oz) butter. Pour on the reserved stock, add the chunks of bacon and the chopped parsley, winter savoury or sage and green leek. Simmer for a further 20 minutes.

5 Season well and serve the cawl with chunks of fresh bread. Alternatively, leave overnight for the flavours to develop.

chunks of bacon

chopped parsley, winter savoury or sage and green leek

Neptune Irish stew

Pierce McAuliffe, Dunbrody Abbey Cookery Centre, Campile, Co. Wexford, Ireland. Irish stew is perhaps the most famous of Celtic soups and stews and what could be more warming on a chilly winter afternoon? This is the Pierce's variation of a classic.

Ingredients

700g (1½lb) totally lean lamb, cubed
450g (1lb) onions, peeled and roughly chopped
450g (1lb) carrots, peeled and chopped
225g (8oz) celery, chopped
700g (1½lb) peeled whole potatoes
freshly ground black pepper
fresh thyme and sage
1 dessertspoon Marmite
equal quantities of cider and chicken stock to cover generously
1 dessertspoon mint sauce

1 Place the chopped vegetables in a generous casserole with the potatoes on top.
2 Season and add all the herbs. Cover with the diced lamb and cover with the stock and cider into which you have stirred the Marmite.
3 Seal with a lid and bake in a moderate oven for 2½ hours.

Serves 4-6

Peat Inn smoked fish soup

David Wilson, The Peat Inn, Fife, Scotland. This smoked fish soup differs slightly from the traditional recipe in that part of the fish is liquidised with the potato and onion to give a more concentrated flavour.

Ingredients

225g (8oz) naturally smoked haddock, in chunks
25g (1oz) unsalted butter
50g (2oz) onion, peeled and thinly sliced
600ml (1pt) milk
300ml (½pt) fish stock
100g (4oz) potatoes, peeled
juice of ¼ lemon
70ml (2½fl oz) cream
freshly ground pepper
50g (2oz) pearl barley, washed
1 tablespoon chopped chives

Serves 6

1 Melt the butter in a pan and cook the onions gently without browning.
2 Add about three quarters of the smoked fish. Reserve remainder. Cover with the milk and fish stock and simmer gently for 5 minutes.
3 Boil the potatoes, drain and mash. Add to the soup with the lemon juice, cream and freshly ground black pepper.
4 Cook the barley in a little water until tender but not 'mushy'.

5 Liquidise the soup and return to the pan. Add the barley and remainder of the smoked fish.
6 Bring back to a simmer then serve in warm soup bowls with chopped chives.

Note: If you wish to make this dish a little more sophisticated for a dinner party, you can add prawns.

fresh herbs,

vegetables and fruit

from the walled organic garden

Pea and mint soup

Eamon Harty, Mor Chluana Restaurant, Barnabrow Country House, Cloyne, Co. Cork, Ireland. Mor Chluana is situated in a converted workers' cottage in the Parkland of Barnabrow Country House. Local man Eamon Harty trained under Myrtle Allen at nearby Ballymaloe House. He believes in using the best local produce, with fresh herbs, vegetables and fruit from the walled organic garden. Note: You may use fresh coriander leaves instead of mint in this recipe.

Ingredients

450g (1lb) peas, fresh or frozen
50g (2oz) butter
150g (5oz) onion, chopped
2 cloves garlic, chopped
1 green chilli, chopped
700ml (22½fl oz) homemade
    chicken stock
150ml (5fl oz) milk
150ml (5fl oz) cream
2 tablespoons chopped
    mint
salt, pepper and sugar to taste

For the garnish

softly whipped cream
fresh mint leaves

Serves 6

❶ Melt the butter in a pot over a low heat. Cook the onion, garlic and chilli very gently without browning for 3 to 4 minutes.
❷ Add the stock, bring to the boil, then add the peas. Simmer for 7 to 8 minutes.
❸ Add the milk, cream and mint and liquidise.
❹ Season with salt, pepper and a pinch of sugar, which enhances the flavour.
❺ Serve in a warm bowl with the softly whipped cream and a few mint leaves on top.

Cream of leek and parsley soup

Emily Cosgrove, High Tide Café, Mumbles, Swansea, Wales. A modern adaptation of a traditional recipe by a very modern café.

Ingredients

350g (11oz) finely sliced leeks
50g (2oz) butter
175g (6oz) potatoes peeled,
    thinly sliced
450ml (14fl oz) light vegetable
    stock
4 tablespoons chopped parsley
175ml (6fl oz) milk
50ml (2fl oz) single cream
salt and pepper to taste

For the Garnish

cream
sprig of parsley

Serves 4

❶ In a large saucepan, melt the butter and gently cook the leeks and potatoes for about 10 minutes to soften.
❷ Add the stock and bring to the boil. Then reduce the heat and gently simmer for about 15 to 20 minutes. Liquidise with a hand held blender or in a liquidiser until velvety smooth.
❸ Return to a clean pan, add the parsley, milk and cream and season to taste. Heat without boiling for a further 5 minutes.
❹ Serve hot or chilled with a swirl of cream and small sprig of parsley.

Parsnip soup

Mrs Ann Barney, Yethen Isaf, Mynachlogdu, Wales, of the Pembrokeshire Farm Holiday Group. Root vegetable soups are delicious, and it has long been in fashion to add a jot of curry powder to spice up parsnip soup.

Ingredients

700g (1½lb) parsnips, peeled and diced
50g (2oz) butter
1 medium onion, peeled and sliced
1 level teaspoon curry powder
1.4l (2½pt) good vegetable or chicken stock
salt and ground black pepper
150ml (5fl oz) whipping cream

Serves 6

1 Heat the butter and fry the onion and parsnips together gently for about 5 minutes.
2 Stir in the curry powder and fry for another few minutes.
3 Add the stock, bring to the boil and simmer covered until parsnips and onions are tender.
4 Put the vegetables in a blender with a little of the stock and puree until smooth.

5 Return to the pan and reheat to serving temperature but do not boil.
6 Add the cream just before serving.

Root vegetable soups are delicious

add a jot of curry powder to spice up parsnip soup

Game soup

Janet Warren, Scotland. This is an ideal soup to make if you have an old grouse or pheasant or some game carcasses. "I usually make it when I cook a game pie and have the bones from the grouse and hare, and the bones and skin of the pork can be added to the basic stock to give the soup a good flavour. It is quite adaptable to the ingredients available, and every Highland housewife will have her own version."

Ingredients

For the game stock

game bones or an old grouse or
    pheasant
50g (2oz) butter
2 rashers streaky bacon,
    roughly chopped
1 large carrot, peeled and
    roughly chopped
1 large onion, peeled and
    roughly chopped
1 bay leaf
6 peppercorns
2l (3¾pt) water

To complete the soup

225g (8oz) turnip, peeled and
    evenly diced
225g (8oz) carrot, peeled and
    evenly diced
50g (2oz) butter
25g (1oz) plain flour
1.7l (3pt) game stock
2 tablespoons sherry

Serves 6-8

1 Break the bones up roughly or joint the bird. Melt the butter, add the game and bacon with the chopped carrot and onion and sauté them all together until the fat is absorbed and the ingredients start to brown.

2 Stir in the bay leaf and peppercorns, pour in the water and bring it to the boil, then cover the pan, reduce the heat and simmer the stock for about 3 hours.

3 When it is ready, strain and leave to cool, then pick all the meat off the bones and pound it to a smooth paste.

4 Melt the butter and fry the diced carrot and turnip gently until starting to soften, stir in the flour and brown lightly then gradually pour in the stock. Bring the soup to the boil, add the game and simmer the liquid for about 15 minutes.

5 Stir in the sherry and check for seasoning before serving.

Kail brose

Janet Warren, from 'A Feast of Scotland'. Almost every region of Scotland has its own version of this national dish. It is important to have a really flavoursome stock for this recipe. Brose is a very traditional porridge soup which dates back to early days when the shepherd or labourer would carry a wooden or leather hoggin filled with dry ground oats. Some time during the day, he would fill the hoggin with water from a brook, sling it again on his back and continue his work. The warmth and movement of his body plus, no doubt, the bacteria in the hoggin, would set up a fermentation which would result, some hours later, in a thick and slightly aerated liquid. Nowadays the brose is made much more quickly. The word brose is associated with a number of different broths such as mussel brose or this kail brose.

Ingredients

1.5l (3pt) good vegetable or
   chicken stock
50g (2oz) oatmeal
salt and pepper
450g (1lb) curly kail (kale)

Serves 6

❶ Bring the stock to the boil, add the oatmeal and seasoning and leave it to simmer while you prepare the kail.
❷ Remove all the coarse stems. Shred the leaves finely and wash them thoroughly. Drain the kail and add. Simmer the brose for about half an hour or until the kail is tender. Leave the pan uncovered so as to retain the colour of the vegetable.
❸ Serve piping hot.

Sorrel soup (cawl suran)

Eluned Lloyd and Judy Cooper, Cnapan, Newport, Wales. Sorrel is a wild plant which, due to the lack of cultivation of so much of Wales, still grows in abundance in fields and hedgerows. Its sharp, acid flavour adds a lovely tang to any number of bland dishes and it can be used raw in salads, made into delicious sauces, or to colour and flavour for a superb soup.

Ingredients

50g (2oz) butter
1 medium onion, peeled and
   finely chopped
1 large potato, peeled and diced
2 good handfuls of freshly picked
   sorrel
600ml (1pt) milk
600ml (1pt) light chicken or
   vegetable stock
salt and freshly ground black
   pepper
lemon juice to taste

For the Garnish

A good dollop of cream

Serves 4

❶ In a large saucepan melt the butter and cook the onion and potato gently for 5 minutes without browning. Toss in the sorrel leaves, stir for one minute, then pour in all the liquid. Season well and bring to the boil.
❷ Simmer the soup for 20 minutes then cool slightly before liquidising or processing to a smooth puree.
❸ Taste the soup carefully before adding lemon juice to sharpen the flavour and more seasoning if necessary. Reheat, and garnish with a swirl of cream just before serving.

kail brose

a very traditional porridge soup

Fish and

Naturally, there is an abundance of seafood in the waters surrounding the Celtic lands, all of which are either peninsulas or islands.

Rivers, streams and lochs or loughs also provide plentiful fish including trout, sewin (sea trout), salmon, grayling and occasionally more unusual varieties like Arctic char found in the deep, cold lakes.

In the past, fish formed an important source of protein when meat was scarce, and salmon and herring were so abundant at one time that farm hands and boat crews would ask not to be fed these fish more than a few times per week. Old photographs of Scottish seaside towns such as Wick and Peterhead indicate the importance of the herring industry in its heyday during the 1800s. Likewise, Wales saw the rise of herring ports such as Aberystwyth, Aberaeron and New Quay, before overfishing eventually took its toll.

Ireland too has a deserved reputation for its seafood and freshwater fish. Along with fine salmon and trout, the Irish, like their Celtic cousins, can offer a wide range of fish from plaice, haddock, pollock and grey mullet to brill, bream, skate and plenty more. Brittany and the Isle of Man have produced such seafood dishes as skate with black butter and Breton lobster or red mullet, along with pickled and potted herring and Manx scallops with butter. And how could one forget Cornwall with its wonderful seafaring lore and towns like pretty Polperro which shout out their fishing heritage? Here conger eel, mackerel, gurnet, and large Cornish crabs make for an oceanic feast indeed – not forgetting pilchards.

That brings us to shellfish. Early records indicate the Celtic predilection for mussels, oysters and cockles. Sadly native oysters are in short supply these days but their pacific cousins, Gigas oysters, have been introduced with great success. Cockles are commercially harvested in the Moray Firth, Scotland and are part of vital cottage industry on the Gower Peninsula, Wales where they are still gathered by hand. Queen and king scallops too are still very much in demand as is fresh lobster, which is being re-introduced in many areas.

shellfish

Today, fishermen still land their catch, including crab and lobster, at the harbour in Aberystwyth, Wales.

Trout used
to be cooked
like this by
the miners

Wrap each fish in
rashers of bacon

a traditional dish with a modern sauce

seared Anglesey king scallops with capers and sage

Martin and Clare Vowell, formerly of Tir a Mor Restaurant, Criccieth, Wales. The Vowells gave up careers in landscape gardening and child-minding to open their fish restaurant. It is not surprising that herbs played an important part in most of the recipes.

Ingredients

16 large king scallops, preferably hand dived, with corals left on (optional) and hard — white muscle removed
light olive oil for frying
salt and freshly ground white pepper
2 tablespoons miniature capers
2 large sage leaves, coarsely shredded
100g (4oz) butter, preferably unsalted

To serve

tossed salad
cooked green beans

Serves 4

❶ Put a small amount of olive oil in a large frying pan and place over a high heat.

❷ When hot, add the scallops, season with a little salt and freshly ground white pepper and cook for 2 to 3 minutes until a dark golden colour.

❸ Turn the scallops and add the capers and shredded sage and cook for a further 30 seconds or so. Remove from the heat and add the butter.

❹ When butter has melted, serve immediately with a tossed salad and lightly cooked green beans.

Trout cooked in bacon

Gilli Davies, Wales. Trout used to be cooked like this by the miners who enjoyed country pursuits in their free time. It is a traditional dish with a modern sauce.

Ingredients

4 good sized trout
1 tablespoon chopped chives
4 slices lemon
salt and freshly ground black pepper
8 rashers smoked streaky bacon
1 small onion, diced
25g (1oz) butter

For the sauce

Greek yoghurt mixed with a little fresh grated horseradish and chopped parsley

Serves 4

❶ Preheat the oven to 200°C, 400°F, gas mark 6.

❷ Clean, gut and possibly bone the trout. (The best way to do this is open up the trout spread tummy down on a board and press hard along the back. This loosens the bones from the flesh. Then starting at the head end, ease away the backbone with the tip of the knife, removing at the same time as many of the small bones as possible).

❸ Put some chopped chives and a slice of lemon in the belly of each fish and season with salt and pepper. Wrap each fish in two rashers of bacon and lay them side by side in a bacon dish.

❹ Bake for 15 to 20 minutes until the bacon is crisp on top and trout flesh cooked and flaky.

❺ Cook the onion gently in the butter for 5 minutes then pour over the trout. Serve with the horseradish sauce.

seafood
Arbroath smokies

Janet Warren, from 'A Feast of Scotland'. This succulent way of curing a haddock originated from a fishing village near Arbroath named Auchmithie. In the early 19th century, the inhabitants moved to Arbroath, taking their skills with them, and by the beginning of this century, the smokie industry had vastly developed. Unlike finnan haddie, smokies are cured closed, tied in pairs by the tail.

Ingredients

Arbroath smokies for 4
butter
freshly milled black pepper

To serve

toast and butter

Serves 4

1 To prepare fish for serving: heat the smokies on both sides under a grill or in a moderate oven.

2 Open them up carefully and remove the backbone. Spread lavishly with butter and freshly milled black pepper, then close up and heat for a few minutes more.

3 Served piping hot, they make an extremely welcome breakfast dish accompanied by toast and butter.

Baked sewin with lemon, cream and dill

Mary Ann Gilchrist, Carlton Riverside, Llanwrtyd Wells, Wales. Mary Ann Gilchrist is one of Wales' most accomplished chefs. Local produce is lovingly sourced and the natural flavours allowed to shine through, as in this simple sewin (Welsh sea trout) dish.

Ingredients

4 x 100g (4oz) sewin fillets
50g (2oz) butter

For the sauce

50ml (5fl oz) fish stock (made
    with a stock cube if you don't
    want to make your own)
300ml (½pt) double cream
handful of fresh dill, chopped or
    1 teaspoon dried dill
lemon juice to taste
salt and pepper to taste

To serve

Hispi (pointed) cabbage or any
    tight packed green cabbage
Pembroke new potatoes with
    butter

Serves 4

1 Melt the butter in a heavy based frying pan and briefly pan-fry the sewin on both sides to colour slightly.

2 Put the fish onto a baking tray and pop into a very hot oven – 240°C, 475°F, gas mark 9 for 3 minutes. Remove the fish from the oven, cover with foil and leave to rest in a warm place.

3 To make the sauce, deglaze the frying pan with the fish stock, and reduce by half over a high heat. Add the cream, dill and lemon juice and cook on a fast heat until you have the consistency of cream. Season to taste and serve with the sewin.

4 Mary Ann likes to serve the sewin on a bed of Hispi (pointed) cabbage which has been finely sliced and cooked quickly in a nob of butter and then the sauce poured round. Cabbage, sewin and dill have a natural affinity for each other. Accompany with a few Pembroke new potatoes, cooked in their skins and adorned with good Welsh butter.

Cod quimperlaise (cabillaud quimperlaise)

Simone Morand, 'Cuisine Traditionnelle De Bretagne'. On the far west of the Brittany peninsula is the town of Quimper, perhaps the cultural heart of 'le Breton'. This is their recipe for cod. In the local town of Dinan, a regional variation would be to serve the eggs sliced rather than halved.

Ingredients

1kg (2lb 3oz) cod
600ml (1pt) salted water or stock
100g (4oz) butter
600g (1lb 5oz) potatoes, peeled, cooked and mashed
2 boiled eggs, halved
chopped parsley

Serves 4

1 Cook the cod in a pan of salted water or stock gently for 10 to 15 minutes. Leave to cool then flake.
2 Melt the butter in a pan, add the potatoes, the cod and parsley. Beat well and season.
3 Serve hot, garnished with the eggs.

Star gazy pie

Kevin Viner, Viner's Restaurant and Bar, Cornwall. The pie is so called because the heads of the fish are arranged in the centre of the pie gazing up to the sky.

Ingredients

6 or more fish (pilchards, mackerel or herrings)
2 or 3 hard boiled eggs
425g (12oz) pastry
pepper and salt

Serves 6

1 Clean and bone the fish and remove any scales. The head must be left on.
2 Prepare the pastry, put the fish in the greased pie dish whole, season well the inside of each fish with pepper and salt, add the eggs cut in slices.
3 Lay the pastry over and pull the mouths of the pilchards through slits in the pastry so that they can be seen.
4 Bake in a hot oven 220°C, 425°F, gas mark 7 for 30 to 40 minutes until golden.

seafood

Cornish portland-style mackerel

Michael Smith from 'A Cook's Tour of Britain', Cornwall. **The sharpness of the gooseberry marries well with the oiliness of the mackerel.**

Ingredients

4 x 225-275g (8-10oz) fresh
  mackerel
salt and pepper
butter or olive oil

For the sauce

225g (8oz) gooseberries, topped
  and tailed
50g (2oz) sugar
2 tablespoons water
1 tablespoon lemon juice
25g (1oz) butter
pinch ground rosemary or bay
  leaf

Serves 4

❶ Clean and split the mackerel, season well with salt and pepper and brush with butter or oil.
❷ Place under the grill until golden brown, turning carefully after 10 minutes.
❸ Place the gooseberries with the sugar, lemon and water in a pan and cook until tender. Rub through a sieve, return to the pan and add the butter and herbs.
❹ Re-heat and simmer for 5 minutes. Serve with the mackerel, either hot or cold.

Warmed oysters with chive sauce

Traditional, Ireland. **In Ireland oysters are now farmed in County Galway, County Cork, County Donegal, County Mayo and County Kerry and are also to be found in the counties of Antrim, Clare, Down, Limerick, Louth, Sligo, Waterford and Wexford.**

Ingredients

24 oysters on the half shell,
  juices reserved
rock salt
40g (1½oz) unsalted butter
4 tablespoon white wine vinegar
a good handful of chives,
  chopped
1½ tablespoons fresh lemon
  juice
chopped fresh parsley leaves

Serves 4-6

❶ Place the oysters on the half shell on a bed of rock salt in a heat-proof shallow dish. Refrigerate until ready to cook.
❷ To make the sauce: melt the butter and add the vinegar. Bring to the boil and reduce until the sauce is syrupy. Stir in the chopped chives, lemon juice, and oyster juices.
❸ Divide the mixture between the oysters and place the dish under the grill for 2 minutes.
❹ Scatter some chopped parsley over the oysters and serve immediately.

Warmed oysters

with chive sauce

Dublin Bay prawn bisque

Terry McCoy, The Red Bank Restaurant, Dublin, Ireland. This is a complicated recipe but well worth the trouble. Terry McCoy suggests you try a good dry chardonnay or champagne with this recipe. However, he loyally concedes that a glass of Guinness is equally good.

Ingredients

4 tablespoons olive oil
½ head of celery, chopped
2 carrots, peeled and chopped
1 onion, peeled and chopped
100g (4oz) mushrooms, chopped
3 garlic cloves, crushed
4 sprigs of tarragon
4 sprigs of parsley
3 bay leaves
3 whole cloves
225ml (8fl oz) dry white wine
2kg (4lb 6oz) whole Dublin Bay
    prawns
a knob of butter
1 tablespoon flour
1 tablespoon tomato puree
450g (1lb) fresh tomatoes
2 tablespoons brandy
225ml (8fl oz) fresh cream
3 egg yolks

1 In a very large pot, heat the olive oil, then add the chopped vegetables, garlic, herbs, bay leaves, cloves and white wine. Cook the vegetables gently to increase the flavour of the stock.

2 Add 2.5-3.5l (4-6pt) of cold water to the vegetables and bring almost to boiling point. Plunge in the whole prawns and bring the pot just to a boil. Remove prawns immediately, and let cool.

3 Heat the oven to 220°C, 425°F, gas mark 7.

4 Remove the prawn heads and shells and place them on a baking sheet in the oven until they are sizzling hot and beginning to colour. Set the prawns aside.

5 Meanwhile, in another large saucepan melt the butter, add the flour, and cook gently. Stir in the tomato puree, the tomatoes, and the baked prawn heads and shells. Add this to the vegetable stock and simmer for one hour.

6 Stir in the brandy and cook for another 10 minutes. Strain the stock.

7 Beat together the cream and egg yolk and add to the bisque. Heat gently, do not allow to boil or it will curdle.

8 To serve, place prawns in bowls or soup plates and pour the bisque over the prawns.

Note: with a side dish of boiled potatoes, this could be served as a lunch dish.

Fillet of cod with cabbage, bacon and Dylan's smooth ale

Nick Bevan, when he owned Chelsea Café, Swansea, Wales. Nick got his catch from local fishermen and treated his seafood with care. In this recipe, he adds a tasty local brew to the dish for a nice twist.

Ingredients

4 large fillets of cod each
    weighing 275-325g (10-12oz)
salt and cracked black pepper
8 tablespoons oil
600ml (1pt) Dylan's smooth ale
    (or other good quality ale)
450g (1lb) cabbage
150g (5oz) cold butter
8 rashers bacon, chopped
chives to garnish

Serves 4

1 Season the cod fillets. Heat the oil and pan fry the cod skin side down first. Turn over and finish under a grill with the skin side on top to crisp, for around 8 minutes.
2 In a clean pan, add a little of the butter and sauté the bacon for 4 to 5 minutes on a high heat. Add the Dylan's smooth ale and the cabbage. Bring to the boil and simmer for 3 to 4 minutes.

3 Add nobs of cold butter to thicken. Adjust seasoning.
4 Place some cabbage in the centre of 4 plates. Arrange the cod fillets on top with crispy side showing. Pour some sauce around each fish.
5 Garnish with fresh chives.

Mackerel in cider from Quimper (maquereaux au cidre)

Simone Morand, 'Cuisine Traditionnelle De Bretagne'. This is a recipe from the Breton poet, Frederic Le Guyader.

Ingredients

6 or more fish (pilchards,
    mackerel or herrings)
25g (1oz) butter
3 shallots or 1 medium onion,
    sliced
2 tablespoons chopped parsley
salt and pepper
600ml (1pt) dry cider

Serves 6

1 Heat the butter in a heavy based casserole dish. Add the shallots and parsley, season and cook for 5 minutes.
2 Put in the mackerel fillets and cover with the cider. Cover with foil or oiled greaseproof paper and cook in the oven for 15 minutes at 180°C, 350°F, gas mark 4.

'Finnan haddie'
smoked haddock

They used to be dried over seaweed which was
smouldering, and sprinkled with seawater
according to Sir Walter Scott, who mentions
them in the Waverley novels

Crumbed smoked haddock

Theodora Fitzgibbon, 'The Art of British Cooking'. Scotland. Smoked haddock is known as 'Finnan haddie' in Scotland and is a famous old Scottish dish from the hamlet of Findon (pronounced Finnan) in Kincardineshire, now popular all over the world. In Scotland it is still smoked slowly, over wood or peat ashes, and this gives it a unique flavour not found when the smoking is done more quickly. They used to be dried over seaweed which was smouldering, and sprinkled with seawater, according to Sir Walter Scott, who mentions them in the Waverley novels.

Ingredients

1 large smoked haddock
 300-500g (12oz-1lb)
fresh white breadcrumbs
salt and cayenne pepper
2 tablespoons melted butter
 (about 25g (1oz))
2 eggs

Serves 4

❶ Poach and fillet the smoked haddock, and then flake it up.
❷ Mix the flakes with half the quantity of breadcrumbs, the melted butter and the 2 eggs, well beaten.
❸ Season to taste and put into a greased fire-proof dish.

❹ Bake in a moderate oven for about 20 to 25 minutes, until the top is gently browned.

Baked whole black bream stuffed

with fresh herbs on tarragon leeks

Martin and Clare Vowell, when they owned Tir a Mor Restaurant, Criccieth, Wales. Tir a Mor won the title of 'Best Seafood Restaurant' in The Millennium edition Red Book awards. This recipe using fish native to the Vowell's corner of North Wales shows off their seafood prowess.

Ingredients

4 fresh local black bream, each
 weighing approx. 450g (1lb),
 scaled and gutted by your
 fishmonger
Anglesey sea salt and freshly
 ground white pepper
A bunch of assorted fresh herbs:
 any 4 of the following: basil,
 dill, flat leaf parsley, thyme,
 coriander, fennel, *plus one of
 the following:* rosemary or
 sage
100g (4oz) unsalted butter plus
 extra to brush

For the leeks

50g (2oz) butter
4 medium sized leeks, finely
sliced lengthways and washed
bunch of fresh tarragon
seasoning

To serve

new potatoes
dressed salad leaves

Serves 4

❶ For advance preparation: melt the butter in a large pan and cook the leeks very gently until softened. Add the tarragon, season, mix well and allow to cool.
❷ Wash and dry the bream thoroughly and season the cavity with a little salt and pepper. Slash each side of the fish three times diagonally then stuff the cavity with your chosen herbs and 25g (1oz) butter per fish and refrigerate.
❸ Preheat the oven to 200°C, 400°F, gas mark 6.
❹ Divide the leeks into 4 and place on one large or two smaller baking sheets.
❺ Brush the fish with oil or melted butter and season.
❻ Place on top of the leeks and bake for 15 to 20 minutes or until the milk white flesh comes easily away from the bones (do not overcook).
❼ Serve immediately with new potatoes and dressed leaves.

This is the recipe they use on Belle-Ile, *the largest and most well known isle off the Breton coast.*

Fish soup from Belle-Ile (cotriade de Belle-Ile)

Simone Morand, 'Cuisine Traditionnelle De Bretagne'. Almost every coastal region has their version of fish soup and the Bretonnes call theirs 'cotriade'. This is the recipe they use on Belle-Ile, the largest and most well known isle off the Breton coast.

Ingredients

1kg (2lb 3oz) selection of fish (conger, mackerel, sardines, squid, ray, cod), prepared and filleted with trimmings saved for stock

450g (1lb) shellfish (langoustines, lobster, crab, prawns, mussels), kept whole

1 table spoon olive oil

pinch saffron

3-4 garlic cloves, peeled and chopped

4 onions, peeled and sliced into rings

1kg (2lb 3oz) potatoes, peeled and diced

6 tomatoes, peeled and diced, seeds removed

parsley

celery, chopped

white of chopped leeks

chervil

1 bouquet garni

seasoning

For the stock

heads, bones and tails of fish

1l (1¾pt) water

Serves 4

1 To make a stock: place all the fish trimmings in the water and bring to the boil. Reduce heat and simmer for 20 minutes then strain through a fine sieve.

2 Heat the olive oil in a large pan, add a pinch of saffron and the chopped cloves of garlic. Add the onions and cook until soft.

3 Add the potatoes, tomatoes, parsley, celery, leeks and herbs. Season and cook until tender.

4 Add the firm fish to the pot first, layering up with the shellfish on top. Cook for around 5 minutes.

5 Present the fish and vegetables on a hot dish, serve with slices of crisp French bread.

6 Accompany the cotriade with a good bottle of red wine.

Breton crab (crab a la Bretonne)

Traditional, Brittany. This dressed crab with ravigotte dressing comes from the famous Brittany port of Saint Malo.

Ingredients

2 large crabs (hen crabs if possible)

salt

dressing made with olive oil, cider vinegar, sieved hard boiled eggs, shallot and mixed herbs

Serves 2

1 Prepare and cook the crabs: bring a very large pan of water to the boil. Add the salt, then the crabs. Put the lid on the pan to bring the water back to boiling, then simmer for 5 minutes. Turn off the heat and leave the crabs in the pot for another 10 minutes before removing and cooling quickly under the cold tap.

2 Separate the claws and pinchers from the body and pick the flesh out of the shells.
3 Mix with some of the dressing.
4 Serve the dressed crabmeat on a large plate on the crab shells, which have been well cleaned and filled with the extra dressing.

seared fillet of wild river salmon

with wilted sea kale and oyster cream

Craig Wood, when he cooked at the Crinan Hotel, Scotland. The Crinan sits by the famous Crinan canal in one of the prettiest locations in Scotland. Craig Wood makes great use of Scotland's famous wild salmon, as well as venison, hill lamb, prime beef and additional local produce.

Ingredients

4 x 200g (7oz) wild salmon fillets, scaled and pin boned

8 oysters

2 tablespoons olive oil

100g (4oz) butter (salted)

450g (1lb) sea kale (or kale if sea kale can't be found)

300ml (½pt) fish stock or water

1 sprig of dill

For the sauce

100ml (4fl oz) white wine

2 shallots, chopped

1 slice of garlic

150ml (5fl oz) double cream

sea salt flakes

white pepper

Serves 4

1 Open the oysters and remove them from the shell, reserving the liquid also, which will help to flavour the sauce.
2 To make the sauce reduce the white wine by two-thirds with the shallots and a slice of garlic. Add the double cream and liquid from the oysters, bring back to the boil, season and set aside.
3 Heat the olive oil in a non-stick frying pan. Season the salmon generously and place skin side down in the pan. Add 50g (2oz) of the butter and cook gently on each side for 2 minutes.
4 Remove the pan from the heat and keep warm, while finishing off the cooking.

5 Next gently melt the remaining 50g (2oz) of butter in the pan and add the kale and the fish stock or water. Cook the kale until it is soft and season to taste.
6 Place the oyster cream back on the heat and drop in the oysters being careful not to boil as this will overcook them.
7 To serve, carefully spoon the kale into the centre of the plate and place the salmon on top. Spoon over the oysters with a little of the oyster cream, and serve.

Trio of native oysters with smoked salmon and auburn herb oil

Feargal O'Donnell, Wineport Lakeshore Restaurant, Glasson, Co. Westmeath, Ireland. In the mid-sixth century, wines from France were in strong demand by the sophisticated Irish monks, and the delivery route was up the Shannon from the sea to arrive here by boat – hence the name Wineport!

Ingredients

12 native Irish oysters
325g (12oz) wild Irish smoked
  salmon
1 sprig rocket
1 sprig parsley
1 sprig basil
1 sprig chives
1 clove garlic
100ml (4fl oz) best quality olive
  oil
cracked black pepper

To serve

buttered brown bread
lemon wedges
Irish stout

Serves 4

1. Carefully open the oysters, making sure they are all plump and moist.
2. Remove each oyster from its shell, wrap in a slice of smoked salmon and replace it in the shell. Place each shell onto a baking tray.
3. To make the herb oil, blend all the other ingredients until smooth and vibrant green in colour.
4. Spoon a little of the oil onto each oyster and warm lightly under a hot grill.
5. Divide the oysters onto four plates and serve with buttered brown bread, lemon wedges and a glass of Irish stout.

seafood

sole au beurre

Traditional, Brittany

Sole in butter (sole au beurre)

Traditional, Brittany. This is a speciality of Cancale, where it is sometimes made without the dusted flour coating.

Ingredients

1 large sole 1kg (2lb 3oz) or 1 small one per person, cleaned and skinned
milk
flour
salt
50g (2oz) butter
chopped parsley
wedges of lemon

Serves 4

❶ Dip the fish into the milk. Flour lightly and salt.
❷ Heat butter in a pan until it froths but doesn't colour and fry the sole until it is golden. Cooking time 5 to 10 minutes according to the thickness of fish.
❸ Serve on a hot plate with melted butter poured over.
❹ Garnish with chopped parsley and wedges of lemon.

Cornish fish pie

Rick Stein, The Seafood Restaurant, Padstow, Cornwall. This is as simple a recipe for fish pie as you can imagine but if the fish is good (and that includes the smoked fish, which must be of the best quality), there is no better dish in the world.

Ingredients

1 small onion, thickly sliced
2 cloves
1 bay leaf
600ml (1pt) milk
300ml (½pt) double cream
450g (1lb) unskinned cod fillet
225g (8oz) undyed smoked cod fillet
4 eggs
100g (4oz) butter
45g (1½oz) plain flour
5 tablespoons chopped flat-leaf parsley
freshly grated nutmeg
1.25kg (2½lb) floury potatoes such as Maris Piper or King Edward, peeled
1 egg yolk
salt and freshly ground white pepper

Serves 4-6

❶ Stud a couple of the onion slices with the cloves. Put the onion slices in a large pan with the bay leaf, 450ml (15fl oz) of the milk, the cream, cod and smoked cod. Bring just to the boil and simmer for 8 minutes. Lift the fish out onto a plate and strain the cooking liquid into a jug.
❷ When the fish is cool enough to handle, break it into large flakes, discarding the skin and bones. Sprinkle it over the base of a shallow 1.75l (3pt) ovenproof dish.
❸ Hard-boil the eggs for 8 minutes, then drain and leave to cool. Peel and cut them into chunky slices and arrange on top of the fish.
❹ Melt 50g (2oz) of the butter in a pan, add the flour and cook for 1 minute. Take the pan off the heat and gradually stir in the reserved cooking liquid. Return it to the heat and bring slowly to the boil, stirring all the time. Leave it to simmer gently for 10 minutes to cook the flour. Remove from the heat once more, stir in the parsley and season with nutmeg, salt and white pepper. Pour the sauce over the fish and leave to cool. Chill in the fridge for 1 hour.
❺ Boil the potatoes for 15 to 20 minutes. Drain, mash and add the rest of the butter and the egg yolk. Season with salt and freshly ground white pepper. Beat in enough of the remaining milk to form a soft, spreadable mash.
❻ Preheat the oven to 200°C 400°F, gas mark 6. Spoon the potato over the filling and mark the surface with a fork. Bake for 35 to 40 minutes, until piping hot and golden brown.

salad of Pembrokeshire lobster

with a cockle and laverbread dressing

Ben Davies, formerly of Llangoed Hall, Llyswen, Wales. This is a wonderful summer shellfish dish. The cool seas around the Welsh coast produce a bountiful supply of shellfish in perfect condition. The dish is a combination of traditional Welsh ingredients such as laverbread (a Welsh delicacy of boiled seaweed), lobster and cockles combined with a Provençale style influence.

Ingredients

2 fresh lobsters, cooked in boiling water for 10 minutes
3 lemons
300ml (10fl oz) extra virgin olive oil
salt and pepper
225g (8oz) Penclawdd cockles
75g (3oz) laverbread, cooked and pureed (now available in tins)
1 tomato, peeled, seeded and diced
50g (2oz) chives, finely chopped
175g (6oz) mixed lettuce leaves

Serves 4

❶ Remove the flesh from the lobster shells as neatly as possible and set aside in the fridge.

❷ Squeeze the lemons and strain the juice. Whisk the olive oil into the juice and season with salt and pepper. Reserve just a little of this dressing for the salad leaves. Add the cockles and the laverbread to the rest of the dressing, then the tomato and chives.

❸ Season the salad leaves with the reserved dressing and place on 4 plates. Divide the lobster in 12 pieces and arrange 3 evenly around each plate and put the dressing with the cockles between each of the pieces.

the cool seas around
the Welsh coast
produce a bountiful
supply of shellfish in
perfect condition

a wonderful summer
shellfish dish

Vegetari

Despite the fact that the Celtic nations are known for their preference for meat-based meals, history reveals that the majority survived on vegetables and grains.

True this was due to a peasant lifestyle which meant a much more frugal diet than that of the wealthy, but nevertheless common Celts made the best of what was available to them. It is no wonder that healthy barley and oats became a staple, appearing in everything from porridge to oatcakes. Today, chefs are making these once ubiquitous grains popular again.

Dairy produce too is essential to the pastoral lifestyle of these nations, and well-made cheeses, creamy butters, yoghurts and clotted creams are produced throughout. Ewes and goats milk cheeses are also on the rise and as with the rest, are utilised in a wide array of vegetarian dishes.

Root vegetables have always formed an integral part of the Celtic diet. Parsnips, turnips, carrots, potatoes, swedes as well as leeks, celery, onions, cabbages and spring onions are all common fare. Mixed vegetable mashes from Scottish clapshot and Irish colcannon or champ are testament to this. The Manx favour pickled red cabbage, while the Cornish, like the Welsh, enjoy leeks with potatoes in soup. Brittany with its obvious Gallic influences also makes great use of artichokes, prunes and haricot beans.

Not forgetting the great Celtic tradition of foraging, we must mention the wild herbs and sea vegetables gathered from hedgerows, fields, marshes and estuaries — sorrel, mint, parsley, wild garlic, nettles, dandelions, sea kale, samphire and vital seaweed full of vitamins and iodine. Dulse, carrageen and laverbread are still harvested and eaten by modern day Celts and appear in all manner of traditional and contemporary recipes.

an

This market stall sells an array of the fresh fruit and vegetables which would have played a major part in the Celtic diet.

Vegetarian
Champ

Sue Farmer, The Bay Tree, Holywood, Co. Down, Ireland. "The Irish tend to cook larger amounts of potatoes for our families than anywhere else, but even if you have some Champ left over from this recipe you can use it as a topping for a pie or just fry it up".

Ingredients

2kg (4lb 6oz) floury potatoes
    (e.g. Maris Piper), peeled
1 bunch scallions (spring onions)
50-75ml (2-3fl oz) milk
50g (2oz) butter
salt
pepper

**Serves 6 or as an
accompaniment to a main meal.**

1 Boil the peeled potatoes until they are very soft, about 20 minutes, then strain and return to the pan.

2 Clean and trim the scallions – don't remove too much of the green part. Slice the green and finely slice the white part.

3 Heat the milk. Mash the potatoes and add the heated milk, butter, a scant level teaspoon of salt and a grinding of pepper.

4 Then some hard work – with a good large wooden spoon or a heavy duty balloon whisk, beat the mash against the side of the saucepan until it is smooth.

5 Potatoes vary in flavour and you must taste your progress, you might well need to add more salt and maybe a little more milk if it seems too stiff.

6 Add the chopped scallions and mix well.

7 Allow to sit for a while so that the oniony flavour permeates the potato. (Some people heat the scallions in the milk but this does not give such a fresh flavour).

Potatoes vary in flavour and you must taste your progress

Allow to sit for a while so that the

oniony flavour

permeates the potato

Vegetarian Fanny's carrot flan

Sheila Allen came up with this recipe while she and her family ran Fanny's Café in Llandeilo, Wales.

Ingredients

1 head of spring greens or 12
    largish fresh spinach leaves
1 medium onion, finely chopped
25g (1oz) butter
1 egg
2 tablespoons double cream
a pinch of ground cumin
salt and freshly ground pepper
225g (8oz) carrot, finely grated

Serves 4

1 Blanch the spring greens or spinach leaves in a pan of boiling water then plunge into cold water to retain their bright green colour.
2 Cut off the stems and any strong veins in the leaves then use them to line a 15cm (6in) flan dish, overlapping, and leaving enough of the leaves flopping outside the dish to fold back over once the filling is in place.
3 Fry the onion in the butter until soft but not brown.
4 Beat the egg, cream, cumin and seasoning together, then add the cooked onion and grated carrot and mix well. Spoon the mixture into the lined flan dish, cover with the overlapping greens, and wrap the whole dish in foil.
5 Place the wrapped flan dish in a roasting tray with enough water to come halfway up the side of the flan. Bake in a moderate oven preheated at 180°C, 350°F, gas mark 4 for 45 minutes.
6 Turn the carrot flan out of the dish and cut into 4 wedges.

Anglesey eggs

Allison Whowell, Goetre Isaf, Bangor, Wales. Most Anglesey egg recipes include mashed potatoes piped as a border around the edge of the dish. This recipe makes a more sophistocated dish which works well as a starter.

Ingredients

4 fresh large eggs
2 medium leeks, finely sliced,
    mixed white and green
25g (1oz) butter
75-100g (3-4oz) cream cheese
1 tablespoon chopped chives
    plus extra for garnish
salt and pepper to taste
50g (2oz) grated cheese,
    Llangloffan, Cheddar or
    Caerphilly

Serves 4

1 Lightly sauté the leeks in the butter.
2 Mix the cream cheese with the chives, salt and black pepper.
3 Place a heaped tablespoon of the leeks in the bottom of 4 buttered ramekins. Add a tablespoon of cream cheese, mix and then make a small well in the centre.
4 Place all four ramekin dishes into a bain marie and put into a moderate oven (180°C, 350°F, gas mark 4) for 15 minutes.
5 Break the egg into the well in each ramekin, and sprinkle over the grated cheese. Bake for 10 to 15 minutes.
6 Serve immediately with a garnish of chives and crusty bread.

Glamorganshire sausages

A traditional recipe from 'Flavours of Wales' by **Gilli Davies**. "A tasty vegetarian sausage made from leeks and cheese. We use Caerphilly today, but at one time there may have been a Glamorgan cheese made from the milk of Glamorgan cows which are now extinct".

Ingredients

75g (3oz) Caerphilly cheese, grated
150g (5oz) white breadcrumbs
1 small leek, washed and finely chopped
1 tablespoon fresh parsley, chopped
salt and pepper
pinch of dry mustard
2 whole eggs
1 extra egg yolk

Serves 4

1. Mix together the breadcrumbs, leek, cheese, parsley, seasonings and mustard.
2. Beat together two eggs and one yolk and use this to bind the mixture.
3. Divide into twelve and roll into sausage shapes.
4. Chill in the fridge for 20 minutes.
5. Fry gently in oil until crisp and golden brown on all sides.
6. Serve with a fruity chutney.

Mix together the breadcrumbs, leek, cheese, parsley, seasonings and mustard.

A tasty vegetarian sausage

made from leeks and cheese

Endive
Chicory

the delicate tapered leaves of this plant stay deliciously crisp when dressed. The word endive in Britain means, of course, the full round shaggy leaved lettuce.

sweet endive and chicory of Brittany

(endives douces de Bretagne et endivettes)

Traditional, Brittany. Chicory in English and endive in French, the delicate tapered leaves of this plant stay deliciously crisp when dressed. The word endive in Britain means, of course, the full round shaggy leaved lettuce.

Ingredients

4 heads of chicory, cleaned
3 tablespoons olive oil
1 tablespoon wine vinegar
French mustard
finely chopped herbs

1 Cut the chicory leaves in two lengthways. Leave the heart whole.
2 Make a vinaigrette with 3 parts olive oil to 1 part wine vinegar. Add a touch of mustard and the finely chopped herbs.

3 Pour over the chicory and serve.

Caerphilly and leek pancake dome

A traditional recipe from 'Flavours of Wales' by Gilli Davies. What could be more traditional to the Welsh than a stack of pancakes. Lloyd George, so it was said, was partial to his pancakes for tea, stacked high and dripping with butter. However, this recipe for pancakes with a savoury filling might be more suitable for supper. It's a great success with vegetarians.

Ingredients

300ml (½pt) semi-skimmed milk
2 eggs
100g (4oz) plain flour
1 tablespoon melted butter

Fillings

a) 225g (8oz) Caerphilly cheese, grated
150ml (5fl oz) double cream
pinch of cayenne pepper
b) 1 large leek, chopped
100g (4oz) field mushrooms, chopped
25g (1oz) butter

Serves 4

1 Liquidise or blend the batter ingredients together and leave to settle for 30 minutes.
2 For the fillings: a) Grate the cheese and mix all but 50g (2oz) into the cream and add the pepper. b) Fry the leek and mushrooms in the butter.
3 Fry 12 pancakes with the batter.
4 Arrange the first pancake flat on the bottom of a heatproof serving dish. Layer up the pancakes alternately interspersed with the two fillings. End with a pancake on top. Sprinkle over the remaining cheese.

5 Bake in a hot oven 220ºC, 425ºF, gas mark 7 for 15 minutes.
6 To serve, cut into wedges like a cake.

Jackie's cooking attracts guests year after year, with dishes like this *homely tart*

Leek and cheese tart

Jackie Dare, Cynyll Farm, Llangadog, Wales. Cynyll Farm is a 77-acre working dairy farm and B&B in the upper Towy Valley. Jackie's cooking attracts guests year after year, with dishes like this homely tart.

Ingredients

225g (8oz) leeks washed, trimmed and chopped
1 tablespoon oil
100g (4oz) Welsh mature cheese, grated
2 large eggs
300ml (½pt) full fat milk
freshly ground pepper
1 tomato, sliced

For the pastry

40g (1½oz) butter
40g (1½oz) lard
175g (6oz) self raising flour
2-3 tablespoons cold water

1 Preheat the oven to 190°C, 375°F, gas mark 5.
2 To make the pastry: rub the butter and lard into the flour until the mixture resembles breadcrumbs. Add enough cold water for the mixture to stick together. Chill for ½ hour before rolling out.
3 Roll out the pastry to line a 24cm (9½in) flan dish and leave to rest in the fridge for half an hour.
4 Fry the leeks in the oil until nearly soft and golden. Place in the flan dish and add cheese on top.

5 Whisk the eggs and milk, add pepper then pour into a flan dish. Decorate with sliced tomato.
6 Place on the top shelf of the oven for 35 minutes, until golden brown.

Skirlie (oatmeal and onions)

Catherine Brown, from 'Broths to Bannocks', Scotland. "I had always assumed that the onion was obligatory but Scottish author from the north-east, Jessie Kesson, does not remember an onion ever being used in their Aberdeenshire skirlie – just suet and oatmeal".

Ingredients

100g (4oz) fat (traditionally good flavoured dripping or beef suet)
or 4 tablespoons oil
2 onions, finely chopped
225g (8oz) medium oatmeal, lightly toasted
salt and pepper

1 Melt the fat or heat the oil in a large frying pan. Add the onion and cook until soft and golden.
2 Add the oatmeal and mix in well. Cook for about 5 minutes, turning frequently.
3 Season well and serve with light creamy mashed potatoes.

Note: Alternatively skirlie may be used as a stuffing for any kind of game bird or poultry. It is also a very good accompaniment to rich meaty and gamey stews.

Vegetarian
Green cabbage with apple and onion

Pierce McAuliffe, Dunbrody Abbey Cookery School, Wexford, Ireland. An unusual but tasty partnering of vegetables and fruit.

Ingredients

1 head of green cabbage, shredded
1 medium onion, peeled and sliced
2 sweet apples, peeled and chopped
50g (2oz) butter
salt and pepper

Serves as an accompliment to a main meal

1 Mix the cabbage, onion and apples together in a lidded pot with the butter.
2 Cook gently on a low heat for 20 minutes. Leave until cooked but not mushy. Season and serve.

Crisp and herby potato cakes

Emily Cosgrove, High Tide Café, Mumbles, Swansea, Wales. What a wonderful way to serve potatoes – not baked, boiled or chipped but mashed and formed into little crispy cakes. This vibrant High Tide version incorporates a mixture of fresh herbs.

Ingredients

675g (1lb 8oz) potatoes, peeled
5 tablespoons vegetable oil
½ medium onion, diced
2 heaped tablespoons of your favourite fresh herbs – a good combination is thyme,
oregano, rosemary and parsley (if using dried, use half the quantity of each)
1 tablespoon plain flour
1 level teaspoon salt
freshly ground black pepper

Makes about 12 cakes

1 Boil the potatoes until soft, then mash and leave in a large bowl.
2 In 3 tablespoons of the oil, fry the onion until turning golden brown.
3 Turn down the heat, and add your combination of herbs. Gently fry for 30 seconds.
4 Add the oil, onion and herb mixture and the flour to the mash and mix well. Season with salt and pepper.
5 Using the mix and with lightly oiled hands, make cakes about 3 inches in diameter and no more than 2.5cm (1in) thick.
6 Using the same pan, add the remaining oil and turn the heat to medium high. When hot, fry the cakes for about 3 minutes each side until golden brown and crisp. Serve immediately.

Green cabbage
with apple and onion

Vegetarian
Red onion, apple and Welsh cheese tart

Hilary Rice, The Huntsman, Dinas Powys, Wales. The combination of flavours works really well, and this tart is delicious with home-made apple and rhubarb chutney. Serve a crisp salad and warm bread along with it. If preferred as a starter, you can divide the tart into eight.

Ingredients

225g (8oz) shortcrust pastry
4 medium red onions, peeled
    and sliced
50g (2oz) butter
4 Granny Smith apples
100g (4oz) Y Fenni cheese
    (cheddar flavoured with beer
    and mustard seed)
100g (4oz) Welsh cheddar
3 egg yolks
200ml (⅓pt) double cream
salt and pepper to taste

Serves 4

1 Grease a 24cm (9½in) flan dish and line with pastry. Bake blind, or empty, in a 190°C, 375°F, gas mark 5 oven (Prick the base all over with a fork and line with foil. Place dried beans in the foil to keep the pastry from rising, and bake for about 8 to 10 minutes. Remove the beans and foil and allow to dry out).
2 Gently fry the onions in the butter until soft, leave to cool.
3 Grate the two cheeses together and core and slice the apples thinly.

4 Place half the cooked onion over the base of the cooked pastry case. Follow with a thin layer of apple slices and half the cheese.
5 Mix the egg yolks, double cream and salt and pepper. Gently pour over the filling. Carefully place the remaining apple slices around the edge of the tart, and sprinkle the remaining cheese over the centre.
6 Bake the tart for 30 minutes. Leave to cool slightly, to finish setting before serving.

Colcannon

Feargal O'Donnell, Wineport Lakeshore Restaurant, Glasson, Co. Westmeath, Ireland. Traditionally, this dish is served at Halloween with coins wrapped up in silver foil hidden in the mash! Be very careful if you try this today.

Ingredients

675g (1lb 8oz) potatoes, peeled
    and quartered
100g (4oz) curly kale, chopped
1 small bunch spring onions
100g (4oz) butter
salt and pepper

**Serve as an accompaniment
to a main meal**

1 Simmer the potatoes in lightly salted water until cooked.
2 Blanch the curly kale in boiling water for one minute. Drain and reserve.
3 Chop half of the spring onions roughly and the other half finely. Add the roughly chopped spring onions to the drained kale and pulse in a blender for 10 seconds.

4 Drain the potatoes and add the butter. When the butter has melted, mash the potatoes until smooth and creamy. Add the kale mixture and mix.
5 Finally, add the finely chopped spring onions and season to taste.

Traditionally, this dish is served at Halloween with coins wrapped up in silver foil hidden in the mash!

Colcannon

Vegetarian
Double baked St Illtyd soufflé

with Bramley apple chutney

Jayne George, formerly of Farthings Wine Bar, Cowbridge, Wales. St Illtyd is a Welsh cheese which combines cheddar, herbs, Welsh white wine and garlic.

Ingredients

100g (4oz) St Illtyd cheese, grated
600ml (1pt) milk
1 small onion, cut in half
pinch nutmeg
75g (3oz) butter
75g (3oz) plain flour
5 eggs, separated
salt and pepper

For the chutney

325g (12oz) peeled and diced Bramley apples
50g (2oz) washed raisins
1 medium onion, peeled and diced
50g (2oz) demerara sugar
1 teaspoon ground ginger
½ teaspoon ground mixed spice
150ml (5fl oz) malt vinegar

Serves 6

1 To make the chutney: mix all the ingredients together in a saucepan. Bring to the boil over a medium heat, then allow to simmer over a low heat until apples are tender, but not soft. Allow to cool fully before using.

2 To make the soufflé: combine the milk, onion and nutmeg in a saucepan and slowly bring it to the boil.

3 Melt the butter over a medium low heat in a separate saucepan, stirring in the flour to make a roux. Gradually add the warm milk to the roux stirring continuously until a smooth sauce is formed. Set aside to cool.

4 When cool, beat in the egg yolks and grated St Illtyd cheese. Season to taste. In a large bowl, whisk up the egg whites until they form smooth, firm peaks, then gently fold into the cheese mixture.

5 Grease six ramekin moulds with melted butter. Pour mixture into prepared moulds. Place the moulds in a large roasting tin half filled with water. Cook in a preheated oven at 180ºC, 350ºF, gas mark 4 for 20 to 25 minutes. Remove from the oven, allow to cool, then turn out of the moulds onto a clean tray.

6 To serve, reheat in a hot oven for five minutes. Spoon chutney on the side of a plate. Place a soufflé in the centre of the plate. Garnish with a few snipped gibbons (spring onions), diced tomato and olive oil.

whisk up the egg whites until they form smooth, firm peaks

Stwnsh rwadan

Allison Whowell, Goetre Isaf, Bangor, Wales. Allison and Fred opened their bed and breakfast in June 1986. Built around 1760 the house has a large inglenook fireplace, contemporary Welsh dresser and a collection of copper and brass. From the outset, the Whowells considered the use of homegrown and local produce important. They even have two beehives!

Ingredients

450g (1lb) peeled potatoes
450g (1lb) peeled swede (or mixture of carrot, parsnip and swede)
50g (2 oz) butter
salt and pepper
nutmeg and parsley to garnish

Serve as an accompaniment to a main meal

1 Cut the potatoes and swede into large cubes and boil 20 to 25 minutes until tender.
2 Strain and mash well with butter, salt and pepper.
3 Finish with grated nutmeg and parsley garnish.

Note: A very tasty alternative is to cook the mixture of vegetables, puree in a mixer and add a pinch of salt, black pepper, 1 egg, 1 teaspoon of sugar, 2 teaspoons butter or margarine, and ½ teaspoon nutmeg or cinnamon. Put in a baking dish and top with brown bread crumbs, dot with butter or margarine and brown in the oven.

Laverbread, leek and potato gratin

Jackie Dare, Cynyll Farm, Llangadog, Wales. An enthusiastic cook, Jackie gives her farmhouse dinner guests as many local ingredients as she can find.

Ingredients

225g (8oz) laverbread
450g (1lb) potatoes (new Pembroke if in season)
450g (1lb) leeks, washed, trimmed and chopped
1 tablespoon oil
2 tablespoons freshly chopped mint (optional) or freshly chopped fennel
25g (1oz) butter
25g (1oz) flour
300ml (½pt) milk
1 tablespoon dry mustard powder
100g (4oz) Welsh mature cheddar cheese, grated
freshly ground pepper and salt
25g (1oz) wholemeal breadcrumbs

Serves 6

1 Preheat oven to 200ºC, 400ºF, gas mark 6.
2 Boil potatoes until cooked, then roughly chop and place in a 20 x 30cm (8 x 12in) pyrex dish.
3 Fry the leeks in oil until golden and nearly soft. Stir in the laverbread until heated through. Add the mixture to the potatoes, mixing slightly. Sprinkle with chopped mint or fennel.
4 Melt the butter and whisk in the flour well. Add milk, stirring constantly to avoid lumps, until sauce thickens. Add mustard powder, 75g (3oz) grated cheese, salt and pepper and mix. Pour sauce over mixture in the dish.
5 Top with mixed breadcrumbs and remaining cheese.
6 Place on the middle shelf of the oven for 15 minutes until brown and crispy.

Vegetarian
Orkney clapshot (potatoes and turnip)

Traditional, Scotland. This versatile mix will happily accompany many stews or fried meats. Orcadian writer and poet, George Mackay Brown, suggests the onion in this recipe. He thinks the idea comes from F M McNeil (well-known Scots cookery writer), but in fact she suggests chives. However, there is no reason why both should not be used.

Ingredients

450g (1lb) mealy potatoes (eg. Kerr's Pinks, King Edwards or Golden Wonder)
450g (1lb) yellow turnip (swede)
1 onion, finely chopped
1 tablespoon chopped chives
butter (Orkney if possible) and milk for mashing
salt and pepper

Serves as an accompaniment to a main meal

1 Peel the potatoes and remove the coarse skin from the turnip. Cut them both into roughly the same sized pieces.

2 Put into a pan with the onion. Add boiling water to cover and simmer gently till just soft. Drain off the cooking liquid.

3 Mash everything thoroughly, adding chives and enough milk and butter to make a light consistency. Season well with salt and pepper.

4 Serve with cheese as a meal, or with haggis.

This versatile mix will happily accompany many stews or fried meats.

Peel the potatoes and remove the coarse skin from the turnip **Mash everything thoroughly, adding chives**

Meat

In Celtic regions meat was a rarity at one time, and the best cuts were often reserved for wealthier folk. When it was available, it would be eaten with great relish and stretched out for a day or two if possible.

Livestock were tended on a small scale by peasant farmers, with the Celts tending sheep, pigs and cattle. Pigs were kept by most houses, and good old-fashioned bacon was a home-cured treat. Although native breeds of sheep and cattle were improved only gradually, Celtic drovers regularly traded with England, 'driving' their herds on the hoof for thousands of miles.

Old breeds would have been relatively small compared to their modern counterparts, which have been cross-bred over centuries to improve confirmation and quality. Yet traditional breeds of sheep and cattle are still very much in existence, including the Manx Loghtan sheep, Scottish Blackface and Aberdeen Angus, Welsh Mountain and Welsh Black, and Kerry lambs and cows. Salt marsh lamb is also a much sought after delicacy, accompanied as it is with seaweeds of samphire or laverbread, just like its mountain cousin which is often served with wild herbs like thyme and lavender.

Offal has been common peasant fare throughout the Celtic lands. Like the neighbouring English — particularly those who lived in the industrialised heartlands, the efficient Celts made use of cheap meat by-products. Offal was eaten out of necessity and a desire to waste nothing – to make use of all edible animal parts when times were lean. Although the modern diet excludes offal for the most part, a number of traditional delicacies have survived and continue to be relished by many Celts. Look out for Irish crubeens (pig's trotters), black and white puddings, drisheen (blood pudding); Scotland's haggis (liver and lights [lungs] cooked in sheep's stomach, with oatmeal and onions); Breton tripe (stomach) with prunes or kidneys and liver in wine; Welsh faggots (liver, lights and melts [heart]) with peas; Cornish liver and bacon with local apples and onions, and brawn.

Glazed ham or gammon, from home-cured meat would have been a treat for peasant farmers and their families.

Cornish pasty

Traditional, Cornwall. The original pasty was a fish wrapped in pastry, made for the Cornish tin-miners to take for lunch. Fish has been replaced with vegetables and meat for very many years. For a family dinner it is usual to mark each persons initial in one corner of the pasty in case some is left over, then each one claims his or her corner!

Ingredients

For one pasty – enough for one person

100g (4oz) shortcrust pastry
100g (4oz) meat (skirt or best chuck steak)
1 onion, peeled and sliced
1 medium potato, peeled and sliced
1 turnip, peeled and sliced (optional)
seasoning

1 Roll the pastry out into a round.
2 Arrange the filling on top. The ingredients should be sliced in layers (or cut up into small pieces) with meat on top, seasoned with salt and pepper.
3 Damp the edges and fold over and crimp edges (crimp by pinching the pastry with the left hand and fold over with right hand, forming a rope like effect on the side of the pastry).

4 Place the pasty on a baking sheet and bake at 220°C, 425°F, gas mark 7 for 10 to 15 minutes, reducing to 180°C, 350°F, gas mark 4 for a further 30 minutes.

Black puddings

Birdie Gardiner, Mohober, Mullinahone, Co. Tipperary, Ireland. This is her own family recipe used over the decades.

Ingredients

2.2l (4pt) of pigs blood
½ of the liver and ½ of the heart of a pig, well cooked and minced
450g (1lb) pork scraps, cooked and minced
25g (1oz) salt
25g (1oz) black pepper
25g (1oz) allspice
1 nutmeg, grated
2.2kg (4lb) well dried coarse wholemeal
sausages skins or casings or ask your butcher

1 Put the blood, minced meat, liver and heart into a large basin. Add the salt and spices to the dried wholemeal and mix all into the blood and meat. It has to be a rather soft, batter-like mixture; if it is too thick to pour into the skins through a funnel, add some of the (hot) water in which the meat scraps (not the liver) have been cooked.
2 The pudding skins should be cut into lengths about a yard long and one end tied securely.

The mixture should be put into the skins, leaving a little room at the end before tying in the middle like a figure 8. A wide-necked funnel is needed to get the mixture into the puddings.
3 Put into boiling water and simmer gently for an hour, keeping them moving in the pot by stirring with a long handled wooden spoon.

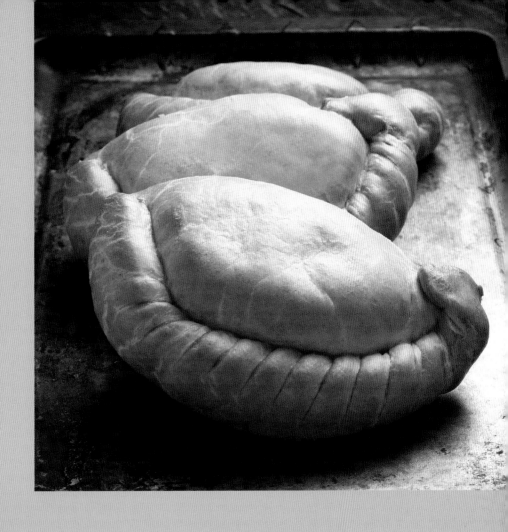

the original pasty was a fish wrapped in pastry,

made for the Cornish tin-miners to take for lunch.

275g (10oz)

carrots,
peeled and chopped

Kerry Pies

Darina Allen, Ballymaloe Hotel, Ireland. "Years ago when my mother-in-law, Myrtle Allen, began to collect old Irish recipes, this was one of the first to arouse her curiosity. Mutton pies, made in Kerry, were served at the famous Puck Fair in Killorglin in August and taken up the hills when men where herding all day. Traditionally they were cooked in the bastible and reheated in mutton broth, then served in a deep plate with some of the broth over the top. It sounds strange, but the old people who remember it are adamant that it was delicious. This is our version. The original hot-water crust pastry was made with mutton fat, but we have substituted butter for a really rich crust."

Ingredients

450g (1lb) boneless lamb or mutton (from shoulder or leg – keep bones for stock)
275g (10oz) onions, peeled and chopped
275g (10oz) carrots, peeled and chopped
2 tablespoons flour
300ml (½pt) mutton or lamb stock
1 teaspoon chopped parsley
1 teaspoon thyme leaves
salt and freshly ground pepper

For the pastry

325g (12oz) white flour
pinch of salt
175g (6oz) butter, diced
100ml (4fl oz) water
1 egg beaten with a pinch of salt to glaze

Serves 4-6

1 Cut all surplus fat off the meat, then cut the meat into small neat pieces about the size of a small sugar lump. Cook the scraps of fat in a hot, wide saucepan until the fat runs. Discard the pieces.

2 Toss the diced vegetables in the fat, leaving them to cook for 3 to 4 minutes.

3 Remove the vegetables and toss the meat in the remaining fat over a high heat until they colour. Stir the flour into the meat. Cook gently for 2 minutes and blend in the stock gradually. Bring to the boil, stirring occasionally.

4 Return the vegetables to the pan with the parsley and thyme leaves. Season with salt and freshly ground pepper and leave to simmer. If using young lamb, 30 minutes will be sufficient; an older animal may take up to 1 hour. When the lamb is cooked, allow it to cool slightly.

5 Meanwhile make the pastry. Sieve the flour and salt into a mixing bowl and make a well in the centre.

6 Put the butter cubes into a saucepan with the water and bring to the boil. Pour the liquid all at once into the flour and mix together quickly; beat until smooth. At first the pastry will be too soft to handle, but it will become more workable as it cools.

7 Roll out two-thirds to 2.5-5mm, (⅛-¼in) thick and line two tins, 15cm (6in) in diameter and 3cm (1¼in) deep, or one 23cm (9in) diameter tin. Fill the pastry lined tins with the slightly cooled meat mixture.

8 Cut lids from the remaining pastry, brush the edges of the base with water and egg wash and put on the pastry lids, pinching them tightly together.

9 Roll out the trimmings to make pastry leaves or twirls to decorate the pie tops.

10 Make a hole in the centre and brush the pastry carefully with egg wash.

11 Bake the pie or pies at 200°C, 400°F, gas mark 6 for about 40 minutes. Serve hot or cold.

Scotch collops in the pan

James McWilliams, Dubh Prais, Edinburgh, Scotland. Scotch collops recipes often call for minced beef, but this recipe uses medallions of beef instead. Either are fitting as it is thought that the word collop probably means small slices of meat.

Ingredients

600g (1¼lb) fillet steak, cut into 12 medallions
300ml (½pt) beef stock
sprig of thyme
2 pickled walnuts, chopped
1 teaspoon cornflour
2 tablespoons olive oil
175ml (6fl oz) port

Serves 4

1 Boil the stock. Add the thyme and pickled walnuts, thicken with the cornflour and simmer.
2 Pan fry the medallions in a little hot oil, 3 at a time for 1 minute each side.
3 Add medallions to the sauce, add the port and boil for 1 minute and serve.

Katt pie

Gareth Johns, Wynnstay Arms, Machynlleth, Wales. Katt pie is an old medieval recipe. It has a long tradition of association with Pembrokeshire's Templeton Fair (12th November). If preferred, short crust or flaky pastry could be used in this recipe instead of traditional hot water paste.

Ingredients

180ml (6fl oz) water
225g (8oz) grated suet
½ teaspoon salt
450g (1lb) flour
450g (1lb) lean, minced mutton or lamb
225g (8oz) currants or raisins
175g (6oz) brown sugar
salt and plenty of black pepper
nutmeg or mace
milk or beaten egg for sealing pastry

Serves 4

1 Boil the water with the grated suet until dissolved. Add salt and stir in the flour. Mix to a smooth paste.
2 Roll out thinly to line 1 large or 4 individual pie dishes (leaving 1 or 4 circles for the top).
3 Fill with the mutton or lamb, currants or raisins and brown sugar. Season with salt, pepper, nutmeg and mace.

4 Place the top(s) on and seal with milk or beaten egg. Pierce to allow steam to escape and bake in a moderate oven 180°C, 350°F, gas mark 4 until crisp and golden.

Forfar bridies

Margaret Horn, But 'N Ben, Auchmithie, Scotland. The But 'N Ben is a family restaurant run by Margaret Horn who began catering over 2 decades years ago in a small fisherman's two-roomed cottage. All of the food is fresh from local suppliers. "We specialise in fish and shellfish but the menu also includes game, chicken, Aberdeen Angus beef and free range duck".

Ingredients

450g (1lb) Aberdeen Angus
    shoulder steak, chopped into
    small pieces
1 medium onion, peeled and
    grated
75g (3oz) beef suet

For the pastry

325g (12oz) plain flour
good pinch of salt
175g (6oz) hard margarine
cold water to mix
egg yolk to brush

Serves 4

❶ To make the pastry: put the flour, salt and margarine in food mixer and blend. Add enough cold water to form a stiff dough. Roll out on a floured board and using a 15cm (6in) side plate cut into 4 circles.

❷ Mix the steak and onion together with suet.

❸ Divide mixture into four parts, and place on one half of each pastry circle.

❹ Wet edges all round. Fold over and press down. Pinch all round using thumb and forefinger.

❺ Brush with egg yolk and bake at 180°C, 350°F, gas mark 4 for 40 to 45 minutes.

game, chicken,
Aberdeen
Angus beef
and free range duck.

gently cook the
beetroot or
rhubarb
with the apples

Aberdeen Angus and Ayrshire bacon meat roll with rhubarb or beetroot chutney

Margaret Horn, But 'N Ben, Auchmithie, Scotland. Meat roll is steamed in pottery (earthenware) jars with a groove around the neck to hold the string. Traditional meat roll jars are around 25½cm (10in) tall and a 8cm (3in) in diameter. Once steamed and allowed to cool, the meat roll is firm but moist and can be easily sliced.

Ingredients

450g (1lb) Aberdeen Angus steak
225g (8oz) Ayrshire middle bacon
100g (4oz) fine oatmeal or white breadcrumbs
salt and pepper
2 eggs, beaten
chopped onion (optional)

Serves 6-8

1 Mince the steak and bacon together.
2 Add everything else, using cold water to mix to a sloppy soft consistency.
3 Fill 2 meat roll jars and cover tightly before steaming. (Use buttered greaseproof circles in the bottom and pressed on top, then cover with foil and tie with string).
4 Place them in a pan of boiling water and steam for 1½ hours.
5 Carefully remove and slice. Serve hot or cold with chutney.

Rhubarb or beetroot chutney

Ingredients

1.4kg (3lb) rhubarb or beetroot
675g (1½lb) cooking apples, peeled, pipped and quartered
225g (8oz) brown sugar
2 large onions, peeled and grated
600ml (1pt) vinegar
1 tablespoon salt
1 dessertspoon ground ginger
1 dessertspoon curry powder

1 If using beetroot boil it for 1½ hours and skin whilst hot. Mince or grate.
2 For rhubarb, wipe the stems and chop into approximately 2.5cm (1in) pieces.
3 In a large pan, gently cook the beetroot or rhubarb with the apples, sugar and onions with 300ml (½pt) vinegar for 1 hour, stirring frequently. Add the remaining vinegar and cook for a further ½ hour. The chutney should now be quite thick.
4 Pour into clean jars. (Sterilize them in a hot oven). Cover immediately. It will be ready to eat when cool, but if you can keep it the flavour will improve. Take care whilst stirring, it splutters and splashes.

spiced beef

Gerry Galvin, from 'The Drimcong Food Affair', Drimcong House Restaurant, Moycullen, Co. Galway, Ireland. "Today the spices simply add a delicate aromatic flavour to the beef, but in the past they cured the meat so that it could last well without refrigeration. I like making spiced beef in summer, serving it with ripe melon and a sweet pepper, onion and honey compote".

Ingredients

900g (2lb) topside of beef in one
   lean piece
1l (1¾pt) water
1 x 330ml bottle of Guinness
1 teaspoon each of ground
cloves, ginger, cinnamon,
   nutmeg
2 teaspoons each of saltpetre,
   allspice, juniper berries,
   crushed
1 teaspoon each of salt, treacle,
   ground black peppercorns

Serves 6-8

❶ Mix together all the ingredients except beef, water and stout. Rub the beef all over with the spicy mixture and cover in a deep dish.

❷ Uncover daily, rubbing the beef in its marinade, for 10 days, after which it should be scraped free of spices and cooked at a simmer, for 3 hours in the water and Guinness.

❸ Allow to cool in its liquid and refrigerate.

❹ Slice thinly when required.

Note: Spiced beef will keep for at least a week. It also freezes well.

Today the spices simply add a delicate aromatic flavour to the beef

I like making spiced beef in summer, **serving it with ripe melon and a sweet pepper, onion and honey compote.**

Faggots

Gilli Davies, Wales. Called crepinettes in France, these balls of offal are wrapped in the pig's caul, or apron, which moistens them during cooking, adding extra flavour as well. In Wales it is traditional to include the pig's fry in faggots; these are the lights, liver and melts (heart), and they give Welsh faggots their special flavour.

Ingredients

450g (1lb) pig's fry (lights, liver and heart) – or use all liver
piece of pig's caul or apron (optional)
1 medium onion, peeled
100g (4oz) brown breadcrumbs
1 teaspoon salt
1 teaspoon freshly ground black pepper
1 teaspoon fresh winter savoury (or substitute sage)

Makes 18-24

❶ Soak the pig's caul in tepid water for 30 minutes.
❷ In a saucepan, cover the lights, liver and heart with cold water and bring to the boil, simmer for 15 minutes.
❸ Mince or process the liver, lights, heart and onion. Add the breadcrumbs, seasoning and sage.
❹ Cut the caul into 10cm (4in) squares and put 2 tablespoons of mixture on each piece; fold and roll into balls. If you aren't using caul, simply wet your hands and roll the mixture into balls.

❺ Place in a greased baking tin and bake for 30 minutes in a hot oven (220°C, 425°F, gas mark 7) until the faggots are well browned on top and the juices run clear when pierced with a fork.
❻ Traditionally served hot with peas and a good rich gravy.

Poacher's pie

Traditional, Cornwall. Rabbits were the easiest of game to poach; no doubt every poacher's wife had her special recipe for cooking these illegal gifts from the countryside.

Ingredients

2 small rabbits, skinned and jointed
1 small onion, peeled and sliced
1 small carrot, peeled and sliced
salt and milled pepper
stock (use a stock cube if necessary)
2 eggs, hard-boiled and sliced
15g (½oz) gelatine crystals (optional)
225g (8oz) shortcrust pastry
1 egg beaten

Serves 4-6

❶ Place the rabbit joints in a pan or casserole with the onion and carrot. Season well. Add sufficient stock to just cover, cook gently until tender.
❷ Remove the joints from cooking liquid, strip the meat from the bones, but leave in largish pieces and arrange in a pie dish together with the sliced hard-boiled eggs.
❸ Dissolve the gelatine in some of the cooking liquid, add the rest. Season to taste and pour enough over the rabbit to just cover.

❹ Roll out the pastry and trim and cover the pie-dish. Decorate with pastry leaves and brush all over the beaten egg.
❺ Bake at 200°C, 400°F, gas mark 6 for approximately 30 minutes.
❻ Serve hot or cold.

Lamb, leek and laverbread casserole

Pat Cross, Whitehouse, Penycwm, Wales. A holy trinity in Wales – lamb, leeks and laverbread! The flavours are traditional but this is a modern dish.

Ingredients

1kg (2lb 3oz) Welsh lamb, cubed (preferably leg meat)
seasoned flour to coat
olive oil
1 small onion, peeled and sliced
4–6 leeks, washed and sliced
3 bay leaves
1 small bunch of mixed herbs
200ml (7fl oz) white wine
400ml (14fl oz) lamb stock
200g (7oz) laverbread, fresh or tinned
200ml (7fl oz) single cream
salt and pepper

Serves 6

1 Toss the lamb in the seasoned flour then brown lightly in a small amount of olive oil in an ovenproof casserole. Reserve.
2 Soften the onion in a saucepan and then add the lamb together with the leeks, bay leaves, bouquet garni, wine and stock.
3 Bring to the boil, transfer to casserole and put into the oven at 180°C, 350°F, gas mark 4 for 1 hour. Remove and stir in the laverbread. Return to the oven for ½ hour.
4 Add the cream before serving.

Mince 'n tatties

Margaret Horn, But 'N Ben, Auchmithie, Scotland. Although haggis is firmly entrenched in most of our minds as Scotland's national dish, mince 'n tatties is up there too!

Ingredients

450g (1lb) minced Aberdeen Angus steak
2 large carrots, peeled and chopped
2 medium onions, peeled and chopped
gravy salt (or gravy browning)
1 tablespoon flour
handful oatmeal
salt and pepper to taste

To serve

Mashed potatoes and skirlie (see vegatarian section)

Serves 4

1 Brown the mince without adding any extra fat over a high heat, stirring with wooden spoon.
2 Add the vegetables and cold water to cover. Bring to the boil, then reduce heat and simmer gently for 30 to 40 minutes.
3 Mix the gravy salt and flour with a little cold water to make a paste. Use to thicken mince towards the end of cooking or alternatively, use the oatmeal.
4 Serve with mashed potatoes and skirlie.

Pan fried fillets of Welsh Black beef

with shallots and red wine

Mary Ann Gilchrist, Carlton Riverside, Llanwrtyd Wells, Wales. To add a real Welsh accent to this recipe, try adding a Welsh rarebit topping to the steaks just before they go in the oven. (See the vegetarian section for Welsh rarebit).

Ingredients

4 x 125g (5oz) Welsh Black fillet
  steaks
75g (3oz) butter
salt and pepper to taste

For the sauce

100g (4oz) shallots, peeled and
  finely chopped
225ml (8fl oz) good red wine (if it's
  not fit to drink, it's not fit to
  cook with)
225ml (8fl oz) beef stock (a stock
  cube will do; alternatively a
  good tinned beef consommé)
50g (2oz) chilled butter, chopped
  into small pieces

Serves 4

1 Melt 50g (2oz) of the butter in a frying pan and fry the steaks for 1 minute on each side. Transfer to a baking tin.

2 Season lightly with salt and pepper and pop into a very hot oven 240°C, 475°F, gas mark 9 for 5 minutes. Remove from the oven, cover with foil and rest in a warm place for a further 5 minutes (this will produce a medium rare steak).

3 While the steaks are cooking, add the last of the butter to the pan in which you sealed your steaks, and add the finely chopped shallots. Cook the shallots until they are soft, then pour in the red wine.

4 Turn up the heat and boil the wine rapidly to reduce to a syrup. Add the beef stock and reduce again by about half, then whisk in the pieces of chilled butter. This will enrich the sauce and give it a nice gloss.

5 Serve the steaks on a bed of mashed potato to which you have stirred in 1 tablespoon of wholegrain mustard, and pour the sauce around. Accompany with fresh, seasonal vegetables or stwnsh rwdan (see vegetarian section).

To add a real Welsh accent to this recipe, **try adding a Welsh rarebit topping to the steaks just before they go in the oven.**

Roast leg of Welsh lamb with

ginger, honey, cider and rosemary

Gilli Davies, Wales. The naturally good flavour of Welsh lamb with the addition of spice, herbs and a little sweetness. The honey, cider and rosemary are local Welsh flavours, while ginger has been enjoyed in Wales since it was brought back by the Crusaders.

Ingredients

1.5kg (3lb 3oz) leg of Welsh lamb
2.5cm (1in) piece of fresh root
    ginger
sprigs of fresh rosemary
25g (1oz) butter, melted
2 tablespoons honey
250ml (9fl oz) dry cider
salt and freshly ground black
    pepper

Serves 6

❶ Peel the ginger and cut into slivers. Using a sharp knife, make small cuts in the leg of lamb and insert the ginger and rosemary. Mix the butter and honey together and spread this over the lamb.

❷ Put in a roasting tin, pour in half of the cider and cover loosely with foil. Roast in a moderately hot oven (190°C, 375°F, gas mark 5) allowing 25 minutes per pound.

❸ When three-quarters cooked, remove the foil and continue cooking, basting frequently with the juices from the roasting tin, adding more cider if necessary.

❹ Remove the joint from the oven, lift out of the pan, removing any excess fat, and pour in the rest of the cider to deglaze the pan. Boil this up well, return the non-fatty juices and thicken with a little arrowroot if you wish.

❺ A well seasoned mixed mash of carrot, parsnip, turnip and potatoes tastes perfect with the roast leg of lamb.

Laver sauce for roast lamb

Laver (porphyra umbilicalis), a lettuce-leaf type of seaweed, is collected daily and boiled in small, family-run factories along the south coast of Wales. It is then sold from market stalls and travelling fish vans by the pound in the form of a gelatinous green puree which has, not surprisingly, a faint taste of the sea about it.

Ingredients

225g (8oz) fresh or tinned
    laverbread
25g (1oz) Welsh butter
1 tablespoon bitter Seville
    orange marmalade
300ml (½pt) prepared gravy
pepper

❶ Put all the ingredients into a pan and heat thoroughly, serve with roast lamb.

The naturally good flavour
of Welsh lamb

Gammon and parsley sauce

Gilli Davies, **Wales. During the last century and up to the early 1950s, pigs were a vital part of the rural economy of most Celtic countries. They provided food in a variety of forms to feed the family from January to December. The pig was tended throughout the year, growing fat on potato trimmings and greens grown in the vegetable plot, and in the autumn it would be turned loose to root out acorns, windfalls and grain left in the fields after the harvest.**

Ingredients

1.8kg (3-4lbs) horseshoe of gammon
1 tablespoon Welsh wholegrain mustard
2 tablespoons dark brown sugar
1 tablespoon Worcester sauce

For the parsley sauce

600ml (1pt) milk
2 heaped tablespoons plain flour
salt and pepper
a good handful of fresh parsley, stalks and all
50g (2oz) butter

Serves 6

❶ Soak the gammon in cold water for 3 to 4 hours, then drain and cover with fresh water in a large saucepan. Bring to the boil and change the water again. Cook the ham at a very gentle simmer for 2 hours.

❷ Remove the skin and cut a lattice pattern across the remaining fat. Wrap the ham in foil and bake in the oven for 45 minutes at 180ºC, 350ºF, gas mark 4.

❸ Combine the sugar, mustard and Worcester sauce and spread the paste over the surface of the ham and bake uncovered for 15 minutes until the coating bubbles. Serve with parsley sauce.

❹ To make the sauce: liquidise the milk, flour, seasoning and parsley. In a saucepan, melt the butter and add the milk mixture. Bring the sauce to the boil, stirring continuously until it thickens.

They provided food in a variety of forms to feed the family from January to December.

pigs were a vital part of the rural economy of most Celtic countries.

Sauté of Pork with apples and Breton cider

Traditional, Brittany. A modern recipe using traditional Breton ingredients.

Ingredients

500g (1lb 2oz) pork loin, diced
25g (1oz) butter
2 large onions, sliced
300ml (½pt) Breton cider
150ml (¼pt) light stock,
   chicken or vegetables
100ml (4fl oz) crème fraîche
2 eating apples, sliced
1 tablespoon chopped parsley
salt and pepper

Serves 4

1 In a large frying pan or casserole, sauté the pork in the butter to seal then set aside.
2 Add the onions and fry until golden. Add the cider and the stock and bring to the boil. Return the pork to the pan and cook very gently for 25 minutes.
3 Add the apples and cook for another 5 minutes.
4 Put the pork, onion and apples on to a serving dish and keep hot.
5 Add the parsley and crème fraîche to the pan and boil the sauce to thicken.
6 Season to taste and then pour the sauce over the meat.

Pan fried calves liver and bacon

Martyn Peters, when he owned Woods Bistro, Cardiff, Wales. Woods Bistro is always buzzing with atmosphere and Martyn Peters served inspiring food in a contemporary setting, as with this simple presentation of traditional liver and bacon.

Ingredients

300ml (½pt) good dark meat
   stock
12 rashers rindless streaky
   bacon, thinly sliced
4 x 150g (6oz) slices calves liver
good quality vegetable oil for
   frying
fresh sage leaves
4 portions mashed potato

Serves 4

1 Boil the meat stock to reduce until it has thickened to a gravy-like consistency.
2 Crisp the bacon under a hot grill.
3 Pan-fry the calves liver in a very hot pan with a little oil.
4 Deep fry the sage leaves in oil until crispy.
5 To serve, pile some mashed potatoes into the centre of the plate. Top first with the calves liver then the crisp bacon, and finally the deep-fried sage leaves. Spoon some of the reduced sauce around.

Game and

The game available in the Celtic lands could hardly be surpassed. Wild heath and moorland, mountainous areas and expansive woodland account for the variety of game available. In addition, there is good, properly reared poultry to be had.

Despite modern intensive methods of farming, happy barnyard hens still exist in the countryside, scratching around the farm as they should. More attention is being paid these days to traditional methods of rearing these birds, and with increasing consumer demand, perhaps chicken will taste as it ought to once again. Fortunately too, a walk past some farms will reveal cantankerous but wonderful geese and busily quacking ducks.

The love of wild fowl and game stems from the innate hunting instincts of the Celt. Naturally, as early Celts were dependent on food available in their environs, they learned quickly to catch and feast on everything from hens, red and black grouse, partridge and pheasant to pigeon, venison, teal, snipe, ptarmigan, woodcock and widgeon. Along with rabbit and hare, cappercallie, wild mallard, goose, plover, squab and thrush, how could one want for more?

Venison was just as important to the first Celts, and later to the nobles who scarcely allowed peasants to feast on such high fare. But today, it is still considered the crown prince of game by many and has, as of late, made a comeback for its healthy image. Now both wild and farmed venison is available. Red deer is the most prominent variety throughout. Fallow, long sought after for its delicate flavour, and sikka deer are also hunted.

Some of the most tasty Celtic game and poultry dishes include Breton partridge with cabbage, Cornish squab and chicken pies, venison cooked with wild berries and wine and simple roast pheasant, mallard and goose. Here you will be spoilt for choice.

poultry

Pigeon pie is a traditional country dish and could be made with other birds as available.

Game and poultry
Braised pheasant with curly kale

James McWilliams, Dubh Prais Restaurant, Edinburgh, Scotland. Pheasant is in season from 1 October to 31 January.

Ingredients

2 pheasants, halved
2 tablespoons vegetable oil
1 onion, peeled and chopped
1 bay leaf
1 branch of rosemary
2 cooking apples, peeled and sliced
50g (2oz) pearl barley
300ml (½pt) cider
300ml (½pt) chicken stock
450g (1lb) kale, washed and trimmed
1 teaspoon cornflour mixed with a tablespoon of cold water

Serves 4

1. Fry the 4 pheasant halves in hot oil for 2 minutes on each side and place in a casserole dish.
2. Add the chopped onion, bay leaf, rosemary, sliced cooking apple, barley, cider and stock.
3. Cover the casserole and braise for 45 minutes at 180°C, 350°F, gas mark 4.
4. Boil the kale in plenty of salt water for 5 minutes, and add to the casserole for the last 10 minutes of braising.
5. Thicken the sauce by pouring in the cornflour mixture.

Boil the kale in plenty of salt water for 5 minutes, **thicken the sauce by pouring in the cornflour mixture.**

Fry the 4 *pheasant* halves in hot oil for 2 minutes on each side

and place in a casserole dish.

Game and poultry
Partridge with cabbage (perdrix aux choux)

Traditional, Brittany. A Breton classic. Using ingredients that are in season at the same time. The smoked bacon and sausage add good flavour, and only careful seasoning is required.

Ingredients

4 partridges
1 cabbage, chopped into 7.5cm
   (3in) x 1cm (½in) strips
100g (4oz) piece smoked streaky
   bacon, cut into chunks
300ml (½pt) stock
225g (8oz) pork chipolata
   sausages

Serves 4

1 Blanch the cabbage in boiling water for 1 minute then drain and set aside.

2 In a large casserole, heat the bacon until the fat runs then brown the partridges on all sides in the bacon fat.

3 Add the blanched cabbage and the stock. Season well, cover with a lid and cook gently for 1½ hours.

4 Add the chipolatas and finish the cooking over a low flame.

Rabbit with damsons

Gilli Davies from 'Lamb, Leeks and Laverbread', Wales. First brought to Wales by the Crusaders, the rabbit was treasured and closely guarded at first but eventually it became a real pest! We already had the native hare of course; anyone could have one of those for a meal, but the rabbit, or coney, was special. Only kings, princes and knights of the realm were allowed to partake of this luxury, and for a commoner to be caught eating coney was a hanging matter.

Ingredients

1.4kg (3lb) rabbit (preferably
   wild), jointed
1 dessertspoon seasoned flour
1 tablespoon olive oil
100ml (4fl oz) red wine
1 onion, peeled and sliced into
   rings
2 cloves garlic, crushed
2 teaspoons fresh lovage (or
   substitute fresh chervil)
2 whole cloves
450g (1lb) damsons, stoned

For the garnish

chopped parsley

Serves 4

1 Dip the rabbit joints in the seasoned flour and sauté in the oil until golden brown on all sides. Remove the rabbit, add the wine to the pan and boil up well.

2 In a heavy-based casserole arrange the onion, garlic, lovage and cloves and put the rabbit joints on top. Add the wine and pan juices and the damsons, then cover and cook in a warm oven 170ºC, 325ºF, gas mark 3 for 1½ hours or until the rabbit is really tender.

3 Serve direct from the casserole, garnished with chopped parsley.

Note: The richness of this dish requires little more accompaniment than a bowl of creamed potatoes or plain boiled, brown rice and perhaps a crisp green vegetable.

Pigeon pie

Traditional, Ireland. This traditional Irish country dish could be made with other game birds, as available.

Ingredients

4 pigeon breasts, cut off the
 bone into thin strips
225g (8oz) lean stewing steak,
 sliced into strips
100g (4oz) streaky bacon, rinded
 and cut into strips
50g (2oz) poultry dripping or
 butter for frying
2 medium onions, peeled and
 finely chopped
1 large clove garlic, crushed
1 level tablespoon flour
1 tablespoon tomato puree
 (optional)
1 tablespoon chopped parsley
a little grated lemon rind
1 tablespoon redcurrant jelly
50-100g (2-4oz) button
 mushrooms
sea salt and freshly ground
 black pepper
pinch of nutmeg and or cloves
225g (8oz) puff or rough puff
 pastry

For the stock

onion, peeled and finely chopped
1 stick of celery finely chopped
1 carrot

Serves 8-10

1 First make some stock by simmering the pigeon carcass in a 600ml (1pt) of water with a sliced onion, carrot and stick of celery. Cook until reduced by half.
2 Cook the bacon gently in a heavy pan until the fat runs.
3 Add some dripping or butter and brown the sliced pigeon and beef in it, a little at a time. Remove the meat and set aside, then cook the onions and garlic in the fat for a few minutes over moderate heat until just softening.
4 Remove the onions with a slotted spoon and stir the flour into the remaining fat. Cook for one or two minutes, then gradually stir in enough stock to make a thinnish gravy. Add the tomato puree (if using), chopped parsley, lemon rind, redcurrant jelly and the trimmed button mushrooms – leave them whole if they are small, otherwise halve or quarter them. Season to taste with salt and freshly ground pepper and a small pinch of nutmeg and/or cloves if you like.
5 Finally add the browned meats, chopped onion and garlic to the gravy and mix well.

6 Turn into a large deep pie dish about 1.7l (3pt) capacity and leave to cool.
7 Preheat the oven to 220°C, 425°F, gas mark 7.
8 Roll the pastry out to make a circle of 2½cm, (1in) larger all round than the pie dish and cut out a lid for the pie. Wet the rim of the pie dish and line with the remaining pastry strip, then dampen it and cover with the lid, pressing down well to seal. Trim any excess pastry and knock up the edges with a knife. Make a hole in the centre for the steam to escape and use any pastry trimmings to decorate. Glaze the top of the pie with milk or beaten egg and bake in the hot oven for about 20 minutes, until the pastry is well risen and set, then reduce the oven to moderate, about 150°C, 300°F, gas mark 2 for another 1½ hours until cooked.
9 Protect the pastry from over browning if necessary by covering it with a double layer of wet greaseproof paper.

fresh lean haunch of
venison, **trimmed and sliced**
into 3-4 medallions per person

Medallions of venison with a wild mushroom sauce

Andrew Huddart, Huddarts, Cowbridge, Wales. Farmed venison may not have the strong gamey flavour of the wild variety but is guaranteed to be tender. This recipe is a real autumn treat, making the most of the season's bounty.

Ingredients

700g (1½lb) fresh lean haunch of venison, trimmed and sliced into 3-4 medallions per person with trimmings reserved
100g (4oz) fresh wild mushrooms or 50g (2oz) dried

Sauce

3 tablespoons ground nut oil
reserved venison trimmings, chopped
4 shallots, peeled and roughly chopped
½ clove garlic, crushed
225ml (8oz) red wine
600ml (1pt) beef stock
1 teaspoon tomato puree
2 bay leaves
2 sprigs fresh thyme
ground black pepper
1 tablespoon cornflour, mixed with a tiny drop of cold water to smooth paste
cherry brandy to taste

Serves 4

1 Heat 1½ tablespoons of ground nut oil in a thick bottomed pan and fry the venison trimmings until brown. Add the shallots and garlic and cook until soft then add the red wine and reduce by half.

2 Add the beef stock, tomato puree, herbs and little ground black pepper. Then allow the liquid to simmer and reduce a little.

3 Gradually add the cornflour mix to the simmering liquid till slightly thickened. Keep warm.

4 Fry the fresh wild mushrooms in a separate pan with a hint of the oil until just soft.

5 Strain the warm sauce on to mushrooms.

6 Add cherry brandy to taste and adjust the seasoning.

7 Seal seasoned medallions of venison in hot pan (not smoking hot) with remainder of oil until golden brown on both sides, best served pink.

8 To present, place a little pile of the wild mushrooms from the sauce in the middle of the plate and a little of the sauce around. Arrange the medallions on top, and enjoy!

Game and poultry
Cornish Chicken pie

Theodora Fitzgibbon, from 'The Art of British Cooking', Cornwall. This is a classic country recipe from Ms Fitzgibbon's fascinating book, published in 1965. With regards to regional variation she says, "In Wales, this pie is made with sliced leeks instead of parsley."

Ingredients

1 jointed and boned chicken, or 4
   chicken breasts, diced
4 slices gammon or ham
8 tablespoons chopped parsley
1 small onion or shallot, peeled
   and chopped
1 teaspoon caster sugar
a pinch of mace and nutmeg
200m (7fl oz) chicken or veal
   stock
200m (7fl oz) hot cream

For the pastry

225g (8oz) flour
100g (4oz) butter
1 egg
water to mix

Serves 4

1 First make the pastry by working the butter into the flour. Add the egg and a very little water, just enough to make a stiff paste. Leave in a cold place until needed.

2 Take a deep pie-dish and put a layer of gammon or ham on the bottom, then a thick layer of parsley, about 6mm (¼in).

3 Lay the chicken on the parsley bed, then a little minced onion or shallot, a little sugar, mace and nutmeg. Repeat this until the dish is full, ending with a little gammon. Season well and add the stock.

4 Damp the edges of the pie-dish and roll out the pastry to the required size.

5 Put the pie in the oven and cut a fairly large cross on the top, so that there is a small opening.

6 Bake in a slow to moderate oven for 1 hour, and when it is ready open up the small hole in the top and pour in the hot cream. Serve at once.

This is a classic country recipe from

Ms Fitzgibbon's fascinating book, published in 1965.

Whole roast herbed grouse

in its own aromatic juices

Colin Clydesdale, Stravaigin, Glasgow, Scotland. "Grouse is only in season for a very short period, so when we can get it, we're thrilled. We like to treat it simply and allow its naturally gamey flavour to come through. Here, only light, aromatic spices are used in the sauce – definitely nothing too overpowering".

Ingredients

2 whole Scottish grouse
   (preferably young and hung
   for at least 1½ weeks)
2 cloves garlic, crushed
½ teaspoon demerara sugar
2 sprigs fresh thyme
2 bay leaves, crushed
1 tablespoon olive oil
25g (1oz) butter

For the sauce

8 shallots, peeled and sliced fine
25g (1oz) butter
1 teaspoon olive oil
1 whole star anise
1 stick cinnamon
1 clove
1 teaspoon orange rind
600ml (1pt) properly made
   chicken stock

Serves 4

1 Combine the garlic, sugar, thyme and bay leaf. Mix together until you have a rough paste, then smear liberally over each bird. Leave for about 4 hours – till the flavours have permeated the meat.

2 To cook the dish, first make the sauce and then marry it up with the bird after about 20 minutes.

3 In a heavy saucepan, lightly fry the shallots in the butter and olive oil. After a few minutes, add the anise, cinnamon, clove, rind and stock. Bring to the boil then turn down to a simmer. As the sauce reduces, remove any scum or froth which rises to the surface.

4 Meanwhile in a hot frying pan, heat a tablespoon of oil and 25g (1oz) butter and sear each grouse on both sides before placing breast up in a roasting tray. Season lightly then cover with foil and place in a preheated, hot oven – around 220°C, 425°F, gas mark 7 (adjust to your own oven).

5 Roast the birds for 5 minutes then remove the foil. Baste them with a little of the reducing sauce and return to the oven. (If the grouse are young enough, they will be sufficiently cooked at this stage. If you like your grouse cooked medium or well done, leave in the oven for as long as it takes).

6 Remove the birds from the oven and set aside while you finish off the gravy.

7 Scrape all of the cooking juices from the oven tray into the reducing stock, then turn up the heat to full. Boil ferociously until the liquid has reduced to sauce consistency. Season to taste then strain into a gravy boat.

8 Remove the breasts and legs from each bird, serving one of each per person. Because of the nature of the ingredients, this dish is equally suited to traditional veg and tatties or the more exotic pak choi and egg noodles.

Michaelmas goose with black

pudding and apple stuffing

Georgina Campbell, from 'Good Food From Ireland'. Goose is associated with Christmas and New Year when it is often a celebratory dish. This recipe includes apples which are at their best in the autumn and winter months.

Ingredients

1 goose about 4.5kg (10lb)
1 onion, peeled and sliced
1 or 2 carrots, peeled and sliced
1 or 2 sticks of celery, peeled
    and sliced
a few sprigs of parsley and
    thyme, tied together
450g (1lb) black pudding
1 large clove garlic
2 large apples, peeled
    and chopped
60ml (2½fl oz) dry cider
salt and freshly ground black
    pepper
sprigs of watercress to garnish

Serves 6-8

1 Remove the goose liver from the giblets and put the rest into a pan with onion, carrot, celery and herbs. Cover with cold water, season with salt and pepper and simmer gently to make a stock for the gravy.

2 Chop the liver finely and mix it with the black pudding, chopped apple and crushed garlic.

3 Add seasoning and enough cider to bind. Stuff the goose with this mixture, being careful not to pack it too tightly.

4 Prick the goose skin all over with a fork, sprinkle generously with salt and pepper and rub in well.

5 Weigh the goose and calculate the cooking time at 15 minutes per 450g (1lb) and 15 minutes over. Put the goose on a rack in a large roasting tin, cover with foil and put it into a preheated hot oven, 200°C, 400°F, gas mark 6. After it has been cooking for an hour, remove from the oven and pour off the fat that has accumulated in the tin.

6 Pour 150ml (¼pt) water or dry cider over the goose and return to the oven.

7 Half an hour before it is ready, remove the foil and baste the goose with pan juices. Return to the oven, uncovered, and allow the bird to brown, basting occasionally.

8 When the cooking time is up, transfer the goose to a heated serving dish and put it in a warm place to rest while you make the gravy.

9 Pour off the excess fat from the roasting tin, sprinkle in enough plain flour to absorb the rest and cook over moderate heat for a minute or two, scraping the pan well to loosen the sediment. Strain the giblet stock and gradually stir in enough stock to make a fairly thick gravy; if there isn't enough giblet stock, make up with vegetable stock or cider as required. Bring the gravy to the boil and simmer for a few minutes, stirring, until all the tasty bits of sediment have dissolved into the gravy. Add any juices which have accumulated under the cooked goose, season to taste with salt and freshly ground black pepper and pour the gravy into heated sauce boats.

10 Garnish the goose with sprigs of watercress and serve with apple sauce, roast potatoes and one or two other seasonal vegetables.

Michaelmas goose

This recipe includes apples which are at their best in the autumn and winter months.

Game and poultry
Howtowdie with drappit eggs

Janet Warren, from 'A Feast of Scotland', Scotland. This early 19th century dish has a very strong French influence. Howtowdie comes from the Old French hutaudeau, meaning a pullet. Drappit eggs are poached eggs; they look pretty surrounding the chicken on their nest of spinach and this is an excellent way of stretching a small chicken to feed six.

Ingredients

1.4kg (3lb) roasting chicken

For the stuffing

75g (3oz) breadcrumbs
1 small onion, peeled and chopped
½ level teaspoon dried herbs
a pinch of paprika pepper
50g (2oz) ham, chopped
50g (2oz) melted butter

To complete the dish

100g (4oz) butter
8 button onions or 2 large onions, peeled and sliced
6 peppercorns
3 cloves
3 allspice berries
300ml (½pt) chicken stock
salt
6 medium eggs
900g (2lb) spinach
2 tablespoons cream
25g (1oz) butter

Serves 6

1 Wipe the chicken inside and out and reserve the liver for later. Mix the breadcrumbs with the onion for the stuffing, together with the herbs, pepper and ham. Bind the ingredients together with the melted butter then place the stuffing into the bird and truss it.

2 In a large flameproof pan melt the 100g (4oz) butter. Add the chicken and onions and brown them over a medium heat. Add the peppercorns, cloves, allspice berries, stock and salt, and bring the liquid to the boil.

3 Cover the dish and cook in a moderate oven, 180ºC, 350ºF, gas mark 4 for 1 to 1¼ hours or until the bird is tender.

4 Meanwhile, prepare and cook the spinach, puree it and beat in a little thick cream and extra butter. When the chicken is cooked, strain the stock into a pan, add the liver and poach it for about 3 minutes until cooked. Leave it on one side.

5 Poach the eggs in the stock, then arrange nests of spinach around the edge of a large plate.

6 Place an egg in the centre of each with the cooked chicken in the centre of the dish.

7 Rub the liver through a sieve into the stock to thicken it. Pour some of it over the chicken and serve the rest separately.

Potted hare with Cork dry gin

Georgina Campbell, from 'Good Food From Ireland'. Potting is simply the local version of continental pâté, it is a delicious traditional way of dealing with the dry meat of game. It keeps well and makes a tasty spread for snacks and sandwiches.

Ingredients

450g (1lb) hare, prepared and jointed
100g (4oz) butter
1 onion, peeled and chopped
1 or 2 carrots, peeled and chopped
1 clove garlic, crushed
1 small bay leaf
600ml (1pt) water
rind and juice of 1 lemon
1 teaspoon juniper berries
sea salt and freshly ground black pepper
1 or 2 tablespoons Cork dry gin
clarified butter

1 Wash and dry the pieces of hare.

2 Melt 25g (1oz) butter in a heavy frying pan, add the hare and turn to brown the pieces evenly on all sides then remove with a slotted spoon and transfer to a saucepan.

3 Add the onion, carrots and garlic to the butter in the pan and cook gently for a few minutes until beginning to soften. Turn into the pan containing the hare, add the bay leaf, water and lemon rind and bring up to the boil. Reduce the heat and leave to simmer gently for an hour and a half or until the hare is tender.

4 When the hare is cooked, remove it from the pan and take the meat off the bones. Put the meat into a food processor with the remaining butter, lemon juice, crushed juniper berries, a good seasoning of sea salt and ground black pepper and the gin.

5 Mix to a puree, but be careful not to over-process. Check the seasoning and put the mixture into an oval pâté dish with a lid, pressing down well to eliminate air pockets.

6 Seal the top with clarified butter, cover with a lid and keep in the fridge to use as required.

makes a tasty spread for snacks and sandwiches

This traditional treatment of

guinea fowl

allows its natural flavour
to shine through.

Roast guinea fowl with parsnip crisps

Eamon Harty, when he cooked at Mor Chluana Restaurant, Barnabrow Country House, Co. Cork, Ireland. Game birds have long been popular country fare. This traditional treatment of guinea fowl allows its natural flavour to shine through. The parsnip crisps are a tasty alternative to their potato counterparts.

Ingredients

1 guinea fowl
softened butter to grease the
   bird
1 parsnip

For the stuffing

50g (2oz) butter
75g (3oz) chopped onions
75g (3oz) soft white
   breadcrumbs
1 tablespoon chopped herbs
   e.g. parsley, thyme, chives,
   marjoram and sage
salt and freshly ground pepper

Serves 4

1 Preheat oven to 190°C, 375°F, gas mark 5.
2 Clean out the cavity of the guinea fowl, rinse with cold water and dry well. Season the bird on the outside and in the cavity. Smear the breasts and legs with softened butter.
3 To make the stuffing: melt the butter in a pan and cook the onions until softened but not coloured. Mix in the soft white breadcrumbs and fresh herbs, seasoning to taste and mix well.
4 Stuff the cavity of the bird with the stuffing. Place in a roasting tray and roast for 1¼ hours.

Test the bird by pricking with a fork – the juices should run clear. Rest the bird before serving.
5 To make the gravy: deglaze the roasting tray with some game stock or chicken stock. Bring to the boil then remove from the heat and pour it into the gravy boat.
6 Peel slivers of the parsnip and deep fry until crisp. Season with salt.
7 Carve and serve both brown and white meat, stuffing, gravy and parsnip crisps.

The gutsy flavour of this chicken pie

comes from the addition

of ham and leeks

– rustic and wholesome.

Chicken, ham and leek pie

Allison Whowell, Goetre Isaf, Bangor, Wales. The gutsy flavour of this chicken pie comes from the addition of ham and leeks – rustic and wholesome.

Ingredients

1 small chicken, or 4 chicken portions
225g (8oz) gammon steak, soaked in cold water to remove salt
2 medium leeks, cleaned and chopped
1 onion, halved
1 tablespoon tarragon and mixed herbs
water to cover, for stock

For the suet crust

225g (8oz) plain flour
100g (4oz) suet
salt and pepper
1 egg
a little milk to mix
salt and pepper

For the sauce

25g (1oz) butter
25g (1oz) flour
300ml (½pt) reserved stock

Serves 4

1. Clean and wash the chicken and place in a large saucepan with the gammon and cover with cold water. Add the onion, tarragon and herbs.

2. Bring to the boil then simmer gently until cooked, reserving some of the stock to cook the leeks (approximately 60 minutes for a whole chicken or around 40 minutes for portions – make sure the juices run clear when the chicken is pierced). The gammon may be removed when tender and kept aside.

3. Skin and bone the chicken and gammon and chop into large chunks.

4. Pour enough stock over the leeks to cover and cook until tender, about 5 minutes. Strain and reserve the stock.

5. Place the chicken, ham and leeks in a pie dish.

6. For the sauce: melt the butter in a thick bottomed saucepan; add the flour and stir for 1 to 2 minutes. Gradually add the reserved stock and stir continuously until the sauce thickens. Simmer for 2 to 3 minutes until the flour cooks out. Season to taste and pour over the chicken.

7. To make the suet crust: mix together the flour, suet, salt and pepper. Beat the egg and stir into the suet mix. Add extra milk if needed to form a soft but not sticky dough.

8. Roll out lightly on a lightly floured board and cover the pie dish, using a pie funnel to support the centre.

9. Decorate the edges of the pie, brush with a little milk and bake for 30 minutes at 220°C, 425 °F, gas mark 7 and then lower to 190°C, 375°F, gas mark 5 for 15 minutes until the pastry is crisp and golden.

Roast woodpigeon with pearl barley risotto, chanterelles and wild garlic

Craig Wood, Crinan Hotel, Crinan, Scotland. This recipe incorporates a panoply of local produce – the pearl barley a thoroughly Celtic grain, chanterelles from the woods and wild garlic from the hedgerows.

Ingredients

4 oven ready pigeon breasts
2 tablespoons olive oil
50g (2oz) butter
1 bunch wild garlic, chopped
salt and white pepper

For the risotto

225g (8oz) pearl barley, soaked for 1 to 2 hours and drained
175g (6oz) butter
1 leek, washed and finely diced
1 stick of celery, finely diced
1 carrot, peeled and finely diced
1 onion, peeled and finely diced
1 clove garlic, peeled and thinly sliced
1l (1¾pt) chicken stock
175g (6oz) chanterelles
1 bunch of tarragon, chopped
1 bunch wild garlic, chopped
50g (2oz) grated parmesan (optional)

Serves 4

1 Preheat oven to 200ºC, 400ºF, gas mark 6.

2 Start by making the barley risotto: melt 100g (4oz) butter in the large saucepan and add the diced vegetables along with a slice or two of the garlic.

3 Gently sauté the vegetables for 2 minutes without colouring, then add the rinsed pearl barley and continue to cook for 2 minutes stirring occasionally.

4 Gradually add the chicken stock a little at a time, stirring continuously.

5 When you have added all the chicken stock, cover with a lid and cook on a very low heat for 10 to 15 minutes.

6 Fry the chanterelle mushrooms in the remaining butter and add to the barley risotto. Take the 4 pigeons breasts and season generously and set aside.

7 Heat up a large frying pan and add the olive oil. Place the pigeon breasts in the pan, seal for 1 minute on each side then add the butter. Continue to cook for a further 2 minutes on a slightly lower heat so that the butter is foaming.

8 Remove the pigeon breasts from the pan and set aside somewhere warm so that the meat can rest, making it more tender to eat.

9 Meanwhile finish the barley risotto by adding the chopped tarragon and a little wild garlic, also if you like some grated parmesan.

10 Spoon the barley onto the centre of the plate and place a pigeon breast on the top along with a little wild garlic and serve immediately, drizzling a little butter from the pan if you like.

Chicken casserole Pont-Château

(poulet cocotte a la mode de Pont-Château)

Simone Morand, 'Cuisine Traditionnelle De Bretagne'. In this recipe, the chicken is cooked whole in the casserole. Alternatively, the chicken can be cut up before cooking, which would reduce the cooking time.

Ingredients

1 tender fresh chicken
450g (1lb) fresh or dried flageolet beans, (if using the latter, then soak overnight)
salt
100g (4oz) butter
2 tablespoons oil
300ml (½pt) good chicken stock
1 bouquet garni
450-550g (1-1¼lb) cepes or mushrooms
550-700g (1¼-1½lb) tomatoes, peeled and seeded
1 clove garlic, chopped
pepper

Serves 4

❶ If using dried beans, drain and place in a large pan with fresh water to cover. Bring to the boil, reduce heat and simmer gently until tender. Alternatively, cook in a pressure cooker if time is limited. Toss in 25g (1oz) of the butter.

❷ For fresh beans, cook in a little salted water until tender and then toss in butter.

❸ In a large casserole, brown the chicken in one tablespoon oil and 50g (2oz) butter, on all sides until golden. Add the stock. Season, add the bouquet garni, cover and cook gently for an hour.

❹ Cook the mushrooms and tomatoes in a tablespoon oil, 25g (1oz) butter and chopped garlic.

❺ When the chicken is almost cooked place all ingredients around. Let it stew for another 20 minutes, making sure the casserole is airtight. Serve in the casserole.

Duck with peas (canard nantais aux petits pois)

Simone Morand, 'Cuisine Traditionnelle De Bretagne'. Nantes is one of the larger cities of Brittany, and geographically, it is at the heart of the Loire-Atlantique region. Nantes, from where this recipe originates, is also the twin town of Cardiff.

Ingredients

2.4kg (5lb) duck
150-200g (6-8oz) strip of streaky bacon cut into lardons
10 pickling onions
2 glasses of Muscadet
250ml (9fl oz) stock
1kg (2lb 3oz) fresh or frozen peas
1 lettuce, well washed and shredded
600ml (1pt) stock made from giblets, 2 carrots, bouquet garni and bacon rind

Serves 4

❶ If time allows, rub the duck all over with coarse salt and leave overnight.

❷ Make some good stock by simmering the giblets with the onion, 2 carrots, bouquet garni and the bacon rinds for an hour.

❸ Sear the duck on all sides in an open casserole. Remove when the skin is golden on all sides – about 15 minutes.

❹ Drain fat, add the lardons and onions to the pan and fry until golden. Add the Muscadet and stock. Place the duck in the centre and the peas around.

❺ Add the lettuce, season, cover and cook for 50 minutes on a low heat basting often.

Rabbit has a fine, mild, gamey flavour and is inexpensive to buy.

Roulade of rabbit with nettle and mustard sauces

Gerry Galvin, Drimcong House Restaurant, Moycullen, Co Galway, Ireland. Rabbit has a fine, mild, gamey flavour and is inexpensive to buy. Nettle tops should be picked only when young in the spring, with scissors and rubber gloves. They make a flavoursome, nutritious alternative to spinach in soups. In Ireland today the nettle is very little used in cooking, although it appeared in old Irish cookbooks. This is a complicated recipe but well worth the effort.

Ingredients

1.4kg (3lb) wild rabbit, skinned and boned
1 egg
2 teaspoons grain mustard
2 teaspoons Irish whiskey
2 teaspoons marrow (or similar) chutney
100g (4oz) young nettle tops, well washed and dried
50g (2oz) softened butter
150ml (5fl oz) dry white wine
salt and freshly ground pepper
12 back bacon rashers
12 shelled pistachio nuts or hazlenuts

For the nettle sauce

100g (4oz) young nettle tops, well washed and dried
300ml (½pt) single cream
¼ teaspoon grated nutmeg
2 teaspoons lemon juice

For the mustard sauce

300ml (10fl oz) single cream
1 tablespoon grain mustard

Serves 4

1 Preheat the oven to 200°C, 400°F, gas mark 6.

2 Prepare the nettle sauce first. Bring the nettles and cream to the boil, then turn off the heat. Leave to infuse and set aside to finish later.

3 Make a savoury mousse by processing together the rabbit leg meat, the egg, the mustard, the whiskey and the chutney.

4 Soften the nettle tops in a pan with 25g (1oz) of the butter and the white wine until the mixture is a green colour and resembles cooked spinach. Season to taste with salt and pepper.

5 Spread a sheet of aluminium foil 45cm (1½ft) square on your worktop, and brush all over lightly with the remaining butter. Lay the rashers side by side on the foil and spoon the mousse across the middle of the rashers like a long sausage. You want the ends of the rashers to be able to fold over and contain the mousse.

6 Sprinkle the nuts evenly on top of the mousse. Spoon the thick nettle mixture along the length of the mousse, on top of the nuts.

7 Place the remaining rabbit meat from the saddle on top, and at either side, of the nettles and mousse. Season with black pepper only.

8 Enclose in the rashers by rolling up the foil into a cylindrical shape and pinching the ends. Roast for 40 minutes.

9 Finish the nettle sauce by bringing the infusion of nettles and cream back to the boil, then flavour with nutmeg and lemon juice. Liquidise, taste and season if necessary. Make the mustard sauce by mixing the cream and mustard with plenty of freshly ground pepper, then reducing to a pouring consistency.

10 When the roulade is cooked, peel off the aluminium foil and carve. Serve accompanied by the nettle and mustard sauces.

Game and poultry
Roast wild venison marinated
in buttermilk

Georgina Campbell, Ireland. Wild venison is a traditional speciality in certain areas of Ireland (notably Wicklow). This recipe comes from Paul Drum, a talented chef and staunch defender of wild venison, who used to run a well-known country house in the South East.

Ingredients

2.4kg (5lb) haunch or saddle of venison
1l (1¾pt) buttermilk
salt and freshly ground black pepper
1 or 2 teaspoons ground juniper berries
a little butter and oil for frying
100g (4oz) smoked bacon, diced
1 onion, peeled and finely chopped
100g (4oz) mushrooms, sliced
2 tablespoons redcurrant jelly
600-850ml (1-1½pt) beef stock
1-2 tablespoons cornflour

Serves 6-8

❶ Marinate the venison in the buttermilk for 2 days using a saddle, 3 days for a haunch. Turn the meat in the buttermilk about every six hours.

❷ To roast, preheat a fairly hot oven, 190°C, 375°F, gas mark 5. Dry the meat and weigh it to calculate the cooking time, allowing 15 minutes per 450g (1lb) for rare meat. Rub the meat well with salt, pepper and the ground juniper berries. Melt some butter with a little oil in a heavy pan and brown the joint all over in it, then transfer to a roasting tin and put into the oven.

❸ Meanwhile, fry the bacon and onion gently in the pan used for browning the meat, adding some extra butter if necessary. When the onion is softening, add the finely sliced mushrooms and cook for another few minutes until soft.

❹ When the joint is cooked, transfer it to a heated serving dish and leave to rest in a warm place for 15 minutes.

❺ Add the bacon, onion and mushroom mixture to the pan juices along with the redcurrant jelly. Stir in the stock and bring to the boil. Dissolve a tablespoonful of cornflour in a little cold water, add some of the hot liquid, then add to the roasting tin. Bring back up to the boil and simmer for a couple of minutes – if you feel the sauce is too thin, more cornflour can be added in the same way, so it is better to err on the side of caution. When the sauce is as you like it, check the seasoning and adjust if necessary.

❻ Serve the carved venison with the sauce and hot poached pears, halved and filled with redcurrant jelly. Red cabbage makes an ideal accompaniment.

Wild venison is a traditional speciality in certain areas of Ireland.

Lady Llanover
was one of the most influential figures in Welsh cultural life

in the 19th century.

Salt *duck*

Lady Llanover, from 'First Principles of Good Cookery', Wales. This recipe brings out the best flavour and will soften the oldest duck. Start the preparation 3 days in advance. Augusta Hall, Lady Llanover, was one of the most influential figures in Welsh cultural life in the 19th century. She enthusiastically promoted the Welsh language and literature and is well known for closing all the pubs in Llanover!

Ingredients

1 x 1.75-2.2kg (4-5lb) duck
100g (4oz) sea salt
50ml (2fl oz) water
2 medium onions, peeled and
    chopped
1 level tablespoon plain flour
300ml (½pt) milk

Serves 4-6

1 Rub the salt well into the flesh of the duck, turning and recoating every day for 3 days. Keep the duck in a cool place throughout the salting process.

2 Thoroughly rinse the salt off the duck and put it into a large pan or casserole. Pour over cold water to cover, bring to the boil and simmer very gently for 1½ hours, turning over halfway through.

3 Stew the chopped onion in the measured water, very, very gently for about 15 minutes until tender. (It may be necessary to press some greaseproof paper down on top of the onions to retain the moisture).

4 Strain off the liquid, blend it with the flour using a whisk, and add the milk. Return to the onions, and bring this onion sauce to the boil. Simmer for 1 to 2 minutes, to cook the flour and thicken the sauce. Either liquidise or sieve the sauce, and taste for seasoning.

5 Serve the duck sliced, accompanied by the sauce.

6 A fruity chutney tastes great with this dish.

Pudding

By the word 'pudding' we mean the sweet course of a meal or dessert – common usage throughout the British Isles today.

However, 'pudding' has its origins in a savoury sausage and the animal guts in which it was once stuffed. Of course such puddings still exist (see meat section), but the pudding has made great progress since its introduction. Once boiled in sausage skin, stomach or a cloth, puddings were eventually steamed in a basin – still in use today. Such traditional steamed puddings were a combination of suet and flour and could be savoury or sweet. Today a lighter sponge steamed pudding is more popular.

Other puddings that have stood the test of time are milk puddings and batter puddings. Of course there is also the uncooked summer pudding full of berries with a bread base – also very popular in the Celtic lands.

Taken in the broader sense – as the dessert – Celtic sweet puddings are primarily made of dairy products and locally grown fruit, as well as wild fruit and edible flowers. Stewed fruit takes us back to the stew pot as a vessel, and stone fruit such as damsons and plums continue to be popular for this method. Pastry of course is also important, and forms the base of many a delicious fruit pie. Whinberry, blaeberries and blackberries, rhubarb, apples or gooseberries are all common fillings for home-made pies – often still made the old fashioned way with lard and butter.

Many memorable puddings exist, including rice pudding which has been a Sunday staple in Wales for centuries; flower or herb ices such as elderflower, geranium and lavender; the Scottish clootie dumpling – cooked in cloot (cloth) and groset (gooseberry) fool; Cornish apple based desserts and junket with brandy; Breton far – an unusual flan; Manx pudding full of currants; and Irish carrageen (seaweed) desserts plus burnt cream. Finally don't forget the lovely oatmeal cream – Welsh llymru or Scots cranachan – for pudding or why not breakfast?

Ecclefechan tart would have been made from local dairy products and grown fruit.
Contemporary versions vary from baker to baker.

Traditional crêpes (les traditionnelles au froment)

Simone Morand, 'Cuisine Traditionnelle De Bretagne'. For this type of crêpe the 'bilig' or griddle should be hardly greased.

Ingredients

100g (4oz) flour
1 whole egg
1 egg yolk
2 tablespoons caster sugar
300ml (10fl oz) milk
25g (1oz) butter, melted
1 tablespoon rum

1 Mix all dry ingredients and add the rum and milk slowly until you have a batter with the consistency of thin cream.
2 Add the melted butter and leave the batter for ½ hour.
3 Lightly grease the griddle, spread the batter out and cook on a high heat until golden.
4 Flip over with a spatula and cook the other side. These crêpes should be thin and quite crisp.

Ecclefechan tart

Jenny Thomson, formely of The Butterchurn, Kelty, Scotland. This dessert is also known as border tart or Eymouth tart. Contemporary versions of this tart vary from baker to baker.

Ingredients

For the shortcrust pastry

75g (3oz) butter
175g (6oz) flour
2 egg yolks

For the filling

100g (4oz) each of roughly
   chopped walnuts, currants,
   and quartered cherries
175g (6oz) raisins
175g (6oz) sugar
1 apple skinned and grated, or a
   jar of stewed apple baby food
1 egg
2 egg whites
50g (2oz) butter melted

Serves 6-8

1 To make the pastry rub the butter into the flour. Mix in the egg yolks with a little water and stir into the flour to make a soft but not sticky dough.
2 Chill for 30 minutes, then roll out to line a 31cm (12in) flan dish. Keep refrigerated while making the filling. Mix all of the filling ingredients together and pour into the prepared flan dish.
3 Level out and bake in a pre-heated oven 190°C, 375°F, gas mark 5 for approximately 20 minutes or until done.
4 Allow to cool before eating.

Les traditionnelles au froment

For this type of crêpe the 'bilig' or griddle should be hardly greased.

Arrange layers of the
oatmeal mixture
and the fresh raspberries in tall glasses.

Monmouth pudding

Oliver Horsfall, Hotel Maes-y-Neuadd, Harlech, Wales. This pudding was regularly on the menu at the Hotel Maes-y-Neuadd in the 1980s when two couples the Slatters and Horsfalls, ran this superb solid mansion house built out of Welsh granite with a roof of slate. Similar to queen of puddings it was originally baked in a large dish but adapts well to individual servings.

Ingredients

grated rind of 1 lemon
2 tablespoons caster sugar
25g (1oz) butter
450ml (15fl oz) milk
175g (6oz) fresh white
  breadcrumbs
3 egg yolks
4-5 teaspoons raspberry jam, or
  100g (4oz) fresh seasonal fruit
  strawberries, cherries, etc.

For the topping

3 egg whites
3 tablespoons caster sugar

Serves 4

1 Add the lemon rind, sugar and butter to the milk and bring to the boil. Pour this mixture over the breadcrumbs and leave to stand for 15 minutes.

2 Stir the egg yolks into the cooled bread mixture and spoon into 4 ramekin dishes.

3 Spread a layer of jam or the prepared fresh fruit over the top and cover with meringue.

4 For the meringue topping: whisk the egg whites till stiff (so stiff that if you turn the bowl upside down they won't fall out), fold in the sugar with a spatula or metal spoon and swirl the meringue on top of the ramekins.

5 Either put the ramekins into a moderately hot oven (200°C, 400°F, gas mark 6) for 10 minutes to crisp the meringue (but do watch them carefully) or bake in a slow oven (160-170°C, 300-325°F, gas mark 2-3) until the meringue is brown and crisp –
about 15 minutes for individual ramekins and 30 minutes for a larger dish.

Scottish cranachan

Gilli Davies, Scotland. "This is a recipe from my grandmother Ethel Miln who served it to her family before the war. It is still popular today and can be adapted to serve with other fresh fruit, although Scottish raspberries are particularly good". It is similar to Welsh llymith.

Ingredients

50g (2oz) oatmeal
300ml (½pt) double cream
sugar to taste
225g (8oz) raspberries

Serves 4

1 Heat a frying pan gently and toast the oatmeal lightly. Alternatively spread the oatmeal over a baking tray and grill gently until light brown.

2 Whisk the cream until it holds its shape but is not stiff. Add sugar to taste.

3 Fold the oatmeal gently into the cream.

4 Arrange layers of the oatmeal mixture and the fresh raspberries in tall glasses.

5 Serve at once to enjoy the crunchy, nutty flavour of the oats.

This recipe is so called because of the

cloot (cloth)
this pudding is steamed in.

Mary Gilbert's clootie dumpling

Mary Gilbert, The Crinan Hotel, Crinan, Scotland. This recipe is so called because of the cloot (cloth) this pudding is steamed in.

Ingredients

175g (6oz) self raising flour
175g (6oz) brown breadcrumbs
175g (6oz) suet
1 teaspoon bicarbonate of soda
2 teaspoons cinnamon
1 teaspoon ginger
100g (4oz) sultanas
100g (4oz) brown sugar
2 tablespoons syrup
350ml (12fl oz) milk

Makes 10 portions

1 Mix all the dry ingredients, add the syrup and milk and mix until a soft consistency is reached.
2 Dust a linen cloth with a covering of flour. Place the mixture on the centre of the cloth, pull the corners of the cloth together and secure with a piece of string.
3 Place the cloth on a heatproof plate in a saucepan of boiling water, cover and simmer for 3 hours, topping up the water as necessary.
4 Take the cloth out of the saucepan, untie and turn the dumpling out onto a plate and place in a low oven to dry off, approximately 20 minutes.
5 The clootie dumpling can be eaten hot or cold and served with cream or custard.

Batter/custard pudding (farz form au froment)

Traditional, Brittany. This dish could be described as a cross between a baked custard flan and a thick batter pudding. Farz form is considered a luxury dish. At one time it was served at weddings, where traditionally a piece was wrapped in a napkin and taken to all who stayed at home, unable to attend.

Ingredients

8 tablespoons flour
6 tablespoons caster sugar
2 eggs
300ml (10fl oz) warm milk
100g (4oz) sultanas (or prunes)
$2/3$ tablespoons of rum or eau de vie
butter for the baking tin

Serves 4

1 Preheat the oven to 170°C, 325°F, gas mark 3.
2 Blend all the ingredients together to make a smooth batter.
3 Pour into a well buttered baking tin. Cook on a low heat until risen and crisp on top, between 30 to 40 minutes.
4 Leave to cool before turning out.
5 Serve with whipped cream.

Puddings

Gooseberry fool (groset fool)

Cathleen McLennan, Clifton Coffee House and Craft Centre, Tyndrum, Scotland. Fools are one of the best ways to enjoy the flavour of summer fruits. Make this recipe when you have a glut of gooseberries – creamy and delicious.

Ingredients

900g (2lb) gooseberries
300ml (½pt) water
100g (4oz) caster sugar
300ml (½pt) milk
1 tablespoon sugar
grated rind of 1 lemon
vanilla essence
2 eggs

Serves 4

❶ Top and tail the gooseberries, and cook in water until tender.
❷ Rub them through a sieve and stir in the caster sugar. Leave to become cold.
❸ Make the custard by heating the milk, sugar, lemon rind and vanilla. Beat eggs and add to the hot milk, stirring over gentle heat to make a custard.
❹ Let everything cool and then fold the gooseberry mixture into the custard.
❺ Serve in dishes and top with whipped cream.

Baileys bread and butter pudding

Pierce McAuliffe, Dunbrody Abbey Cookery School, Wexford, Ireland. There aren't many people who dislike a drop of Baileys. When added to a traditional pudding like this one, it provides creaminess and luxury! Barm brack is a speckled and fermented Irish bread.

Ingredients

1 small brack loaf – or any rich tea bread
50g (2oz) butter
4 eggs
100g (4oz) caster sugar
600ml (1pt) milk
a good glassful of Bailey's Irish Cream liqueur
whole nutmeg to grate

Serves 4

❶ Cut the loaf. Butter the slices liberally. Cut into triangles.
❷ Place in a buttered dish until filled. Mix the eggs, sugar and milk together. Add the Baileys and pour over the brack. Grate fresh nutmeg over the top.
❸ Bake at 180°C, 350°F, gas mark 4 for 20 to 30 minutes until set.

Make this recipe when you have a

glut of gooseberries
— creamy and delicious.

Irish moss ginger jelly

Feargal O'Donnell, Wineport Lakeshore Restaurant, Glasson, Co. Westmeath, Ireland.
Carrageen moss is a natural food (seaweed) collected from unpolluted waters of the Atlantic.
It contains various minerals and vitamins, and due to its high iodine content, is used as an
aid to slimming. You can find it in its dried form at many health food and specialist shops.
Irish Mist is an Irish whiskey liqueur – often taken as an after dinner digestive.

Ingredients

25g (1oz) carrageen moss
600ml (1pt) water
50g (2oz) sugar
¼ teaspoon ginger, freshly
    grated
zest of 1 lemon
150ml (5fl oz) cream
1 egg white

To serve

orange segments
Irish Mist to flambé
fresh mint

Serves 4

1 Simmer the carrageen moss for three minutes in the water with the sugar, ginger and lemon zest. Strain into a bowl and leave to cool.

2 Whip the cream and egg white separately until stiff, then combine together.

3 Add the two mixtures together and heat until almost at boiling point.

4 Pour into small individual moulds lined with cling film. Chill for one hour.

5 To serve, turn each mould out onto a serving plate and decorate with orange segments flambéed with Irish Mist and fresh mint.

Blackcurrant and elderflower cream

Jane Heard, Tregynon Country Farmhouse Hotel, Wales. The following recipe comes from Peter and Jane Heard's 1994 anthology of food and verse, 'Dining with Angels'.

Ingredients

100g (4oz) fresh blackcurrants
    (or frozen if fresh not
    available)
2 tablespoons elderflower
    essence
1 tablespoon caster sugar
150ml (¼pt) double cream
2 tablespoons lemon juice

Serves 4

1 Pour the elderflower essence onto the blackcurrants and leave to marinate for at least an hour. Add a little sugar and cook in a saucepan on a gentle heat or in the microwave (covered, or it goes everywhere!) until the blackcurrants are soft. Leave the blackcurrants to cool.

2 Whisk the cream until it will hold in soft peaks and gently whip in the blackcurrant mixture, adding lemon juice to taste. Add more sugar if you prefer a sweeter dessert.

3 Pour into tall glasses and garnish with a mint leaf, cape gooseberry or similar garnish.

Elderflower sorbet

Allison Whowell, Goetre Isaf, Bangor, Wales. Elderflowers blossom in May and should be picked in profusion so that bottles and bottles of elderflower cordial can be made for use later in the year. This syrup brings a delightfully flowery flavour to any number of sweet dishes.

Ingredients

6 tablespoons elderflower cordial
450ml (¾pt) apple juice or
   water
juice and zest of 1 lemon
125g (5oz) caster sugar
1 egg white

To serve

twist of lemon
lemon zest
almond or shortbread biscuit

1. Bring the apple juice to the boil with the juice of 1 lemon, lemon zest and 100g (4oz) of caster sugar.
2. Leave to cool and then stir in the elderflower cordial. Transfer to a suitable container. Deep freeze for 2 hours.
3. Stir very well to break up ice crystals.
4. Beat the egg white to peaks and add 25g (1oz) of caster sugar. Beat to meringue consistency. Combine with the frozen mixture and mix very well. Freeze and again break up crystals after another 2 hours or so.
5. Serve with a twist of lemon or lemon zest, and an almond or shortbread biscuit.

Brown bread ice cream

Pierce McAuliffe, Dunbrody Abbey Cookery Centre, Campile, Co. Wexford, Ireland. A fine example of the simple and delicious food prepared at Dunbrody Abbey.

Ingredients

150g (6oz) wholemeal or wheaten
   brown bread
300ml (½pt) double cream
150ml (¼pt) single cream
100g (4oz) caster sugar
2 eggs separated
1 teaspoon vanilla essence
2 tablespoons Baileys Irish
   Cream liqueur

Serves 4

1. Toast the bread, let it cool then blend to make breadcrumbs.
2. Whip the creams together with the sugar, egg yolks, vanilla essence and Baileys cream. Fold in the crumbs.
3. Whisk the egg whites very stiffly and fold gently into the ice cream. Spoon the mixture into a rigid plastic box. Cover with a lid.
4. Freeze until firm, at least 4 hours.

Puddings

Snowdonia pudding

Gilli Davies, Wales. This is a suet pudding created for the hearty appetites of those walking in the north Welsh mountains of Snowdonia.

Ingredients

100g (4oz) suet (animal or
    vegetarian)
100g (4oz) fresh white or brown
    breadcrumbs
1 tablespoon cornflour or ground
    rice
pinch of salt
finely grated rind of 1 lemon
2 tablespoons lemon or orange
    marmalade
3 tablespoons caster sugar
3 well beaten eggs
3 tablespoons seedless raisins
a little butter

For the wine sauce

2 tablespoons granulated sugar
½ lemon rind in one piece
2 tablespoons water
1 tablespoon cornflour
1 tablespoon butter
150ml (¼pt) Madeira, sherry
    or home-made sweet wine

Serves 6

1 Grease a 1.2l (2pt) basin with the butter and press as many raisins on to the sides as will stick.

2 Mix together the suet, breadcrumbs, cornflour and salt, then add the grated lemon rind, marmalade and sugar.

3 Add the beaten eggs and any remaining raisins. Carefully spoon the mixture into the basin.

4 Cover and steam for 50 to 60 minutes or microwave on high for 5 minutes. Turn out onto a warm plate and serve with the wine sauce.

5 For the wine sauce: Boil the sugar, lemon rind and water for 2 minutes then remove the rind. Mix the cornflour into the butter and stir into the syrup then add the wine and let it simmer for a few minutes to thicken. Serve in a small jug with the steaming hot pudding.

Cornish junket

Traditional, Cornwall.

Ingredients

300ml (½pt) fresh milk
300ml (½pt) Cornish cream
1 teaspoon of rennet
50g (2oz) sugar
half a nutmeg, grated

Serves 4

1 Mix the milk and cream together and sprinkle in the sugar.

2 Slowly warm until the sugar is dissolved and the liquid no more than blood heat.

3 Stir in the rennet, pour immediately into a large shallow serving dish and leave in the kitchen atmosphere to set.

Suet pudding

created for the hearty appetites of those walking in the north Welsh mountains of Snowdonia.

Welsh honey ice cream

The most natural of sweeteners, honey adds a special flavour to ice cream.

Welsh honey ice cream

Joyce Hart, previous owner of Glasfryn Guest House and Restaurant, Brechfa, Wales. One can well imagine the Druids preparing honey and today in Wales there is a great choice of flavours available. The most natural of sweeteners, honey adds a special flavour to ice cream.

Ingredients

250g (9oz) runny Welsh honey
8 egg yolks
50g (2oz) caster sugar
600ml (1pt) single cream
pine nuts to garnish

Serves 6

1 Beat together the egg yolks and sugar until pale.

2 Heat the cream until just below boiling point and stir into the egg mixture. Pour the mixture into a small pan, heat very gently – preferably over a pan of boiling water (bain marie) – and stir until thick. This will take about 10 minutes.

3 Add the honey and stir well. Remove from the heat and cool.

4 Pour into a container and freeze for about 1½ hours. Remove from the freezer and beat the ice cream to stop any crystals from forming. Repeat this process 3 or 4 times every hour. Cover with a layer of parchment paper and a secure lid.

5 Freeze for approximately 3 hours. Remove the ice cream, and place in a refrigerator 30 minutes before serving. Garnish with pine nuts and an extra spoon of honey.

Carrageen soufflé

Georgina Campbell, Ireland. This is a lighter, fluffier version of carrageen pudding and looks more festive for a special occasion. It is flavoured with Irish Mist, a liqueur popular in cooking which features on many restaurant menus.

Ingredients

300ml (1pt) milk
12g (½oz) carrageen
25g (1oz) caster sugar
1 egg
150ml (5fl oz) cream
1 tablespoon Irish Mist liqueur, or to taste
whipped sweetened cream and toasted flaked almonds to decorate

Serves 4

1 Prepare a 600ml (1pt) soufflé dish by tying a band of double baking parchment around the outside of the mould. The paper should come about 5cm (2in) above the top of the dish.

2 Remove any discoloured parts from the carrageen and steep it in water for 10 to 15 minutes, then drain well and put into a saucepan with the milk.

3 Bring up to boiling point and simmer very gently for about 10 minutes until it coats the back of a wooden spoon.

4 Whisk the egg yolk and liqueur with the sugar and strain the carrageen in to it. Whisk well until it begins to set.

5 Whisk the cream lightly and whisk the egg white stiffly.

6 Fold them both into the carrageen mixture and pour into the prepared soufflé dish, or alternatively, into individual glasses.

7 Chill until set and carefully remove the paper, then decorate with whipped cream and toasted almonds.

Puddings
Whinberry and apple pie

A traditional recipe from 'Flavours of Wales', by **Gilli Davies**. Whinberries in Wales, myrtleberries or blaeberries elsewhere, but definitely not blueberries! These small purplish berries which appear in late July and August grow on low rather prickly bushes in the Welsh hills and were a great favourite with the miners who would pick them in the late afternoon after a day down the pit. They are available in bottles out of season, or can be substituted with blackcurrants.

Ingredients

For the pastry

350g (12oz) plain flour
175g (6oz) butter and lard mixed
100g (4oz) caster sugar
1 egg yolk
a few tablespoons cold water
    to mix

For the filling

450g (1lb) fresh whinberries,
    picked over
5 large cooking apples
75g (3oz) caster sugar
pinch of cinnamon
juice of half a lemon
caster sugar to glaze

Serves 6

1 To make the pastry: rub the fat into the flour until it looks like breadcrumbs. Then stir in the sugar. Add the egg yolk and enough cold water to make a firm dough. Leave to rest in the fridge wrapped in greaseproof paper.

2 To make the filling: peel and slice the cooking apples and cook in a saucepan with the sugar, cinnamon and lemon juice. The apples should be soft but not lose their shape or mush to a puree. Leave to cool.

3 Roll the pastry out to line an 20cm (8in) flan tin, reserving about a third for the lid.

4 Spoon in layers of the apples and whinberries. Cover the pie with the lid, brush with cold water and sprinkle with sugar.

5 Bake at 190°C, 375°F, gas mark 5 for 25 minutes or until golden brown. Serve with fresh cream or a light custard.

Whinberry, a great favourite with the miners

who would pick them in the late afternoon after a day down the pit.

Rice pudding

must conjure up memories for everyone.

In Wales, the tradition was to serve rice pudding after a roast, baking the pudding underneath the meat made good use of the lit oven and provided the family with a favourite treat.

Welsh rice pudding

Ken Goody, formerly of the Cemlyn Restaurant, Harlech, Wales. Rice pudding must conjure up memories for everyone. They may be of loathing, left over from schooldays, or pure pleasure in recalling that sweet, comforting smell synonymous with Sunday lunch. In Wales, the tradition was to serve rice pudding after a roast, baking the pudding underneath the meat made good use of the lit oven and provided the family with a favourite treat.

Ingredients

300ml (½pt) milk
300ml (½pt) single cream
½ vanilla pod
50g (2oz) round pudding rice
25g (1oz) caster sugar
50g (2oz) unsalted butter
2 whole eggs
2 egg yolks
2 tablespoons whisky
100g (4oz) dark, coarse-cut marmalade
25g (1oz) demerara sugar (optional)

For the brulée

50g (2oz) caster sugar

Serves 4

1 Preheat the oven to 180°C, 350°F, gas mark 4.
2 In a saucepan, bring the milk, cream and vanilla pod to the boil. Add the rice, stir and then simmer gently for 20 minutes until the rice is tender. Stir in the sugar. Remove the vanilla pod, which may be dried and used again.
3 Using some of the butter, grease a 1.2l (2pt) bowl or pie dish.
4 Beat the 2 whole eggs and 2 yolks with the whisky and marmalade and stir into the rice mixture. Pour into the dish and dot the top with the remaining butter (and a little demerara sugar if you are serving the rice pudding hot).
5 Bake for 30 minutes.
6 Either serve the rice pudding hot, straight from the oven, or leave to cool and serve as a rice brulée.
7 To make rice brulée: preheat the grill to its hottest; dust the cool rice pudding with caster sugar and grill until a crisp caramel forms on top. Chill before serving.

Manx batter pudding

Traditional, Isle of Man.

Ingredients

100g (4oz) plain flour
2 eggs, beaten
275ml (½pt) milk
25g (1oz) currants
50g (2oz) caster sugar

Serves 4

1 Pour the flour into a mixing bowl. Make a well in the centre, add the eggs and mix in.
2 Slowly add the milk to make a smooth batter. Beat well and stir in the currants and sugar.
3 Pour into a greased pudding basin, cover and steam for 1 to ½ hours.
4 Serve hot.

Baking

The griddle, like the stewpot, is the very essence of Celtic cooking. A handle or chain would allow the griddle to be suspended over an open fire fuelled by peat, coal or wood.

Alternatively, the large cast iron pot with lid, which was used for all manner of cooking, acted as an oven once covered in the embers of the fire. This too had indigenous names e.g. the Irish bastible or the Welsh pot oven, and was used for baking certain types of bread, fuelled in the same manner or with whatever was available in the locality e.g. gorse, straw or culm. Finally, the bread or wall oven, which can still be witnessed in old houses today, was also used for baking.

There are many local names for the griddle. Called a bakestone, girdle, maen, it gave the Celts a reliable means of producing unleavened and yeasted breads and oat biscuits, and took the place of the oven.

Plain or buckwheat (sarrasin) pancakes, griddle cakes, oaten bread and oatcakes, scones and farls, barley meal bread, wholemeal soda breads and even Indian meal (yellow meal) and rye breads are made –some very localised, but most a product of all of the nations. Buttermilk or soured milk adds moisture and lightness to many breads, while potatoes lend their floury texture to savoury griddlecakes. Currants, raisins, tea and treacle make their appearance in sweet loaves, while apples are added in and soft fruit used as a topping for pancakes. The list goes on...

The Celts developed reliable means of producing unleaved bread, biscuits, griddle cakes, scones and shortbread.

Easily identified by its almond scattered surface

a special tea cake often made for festive occasions.

Bara brith

Gilli Davies, from 'Lamb, Leeks and Laverbread', Wales. This is literally translated as speckled bread. Once a week the stove was lit for baking day and from dawn to dusk the smell of fresh bread wafted out of the kitchen. As the heat began to fade in the stove so a handful of currants was added to the last of the bread dough and this speckled bread became a treat.

Ingredients

450g (1lb) mixed dried fruit
300ml (½pt) cold tea
2 tablespoons marmalade
1 egg, beaten
6 tablespoons soft brown sugar
1 teaspoon mixed spice
450g (1lb) self-raising flour
honey to glaze

1. Soak the fruit overnight in the tea.
2. Next day, mix in the marmalade, egg, sugar, spice and flour.
3. Spoon into a greased 900g (2lb) loaf tin and bake in a warm oven (170ºC, 325ºF, gas mark 3) for 1¾ hours or until the centre is cooked through. Check from time to time that the top doesn't brown too much, and cover with a sheet of foil or move down a shelf in the oven if necessary.
4. Once cooked, leave the bara brith to stand for 5 minutes then tip out of the tin on to a cooling tray. Using a pastry brush, glaze the top with honey.
5. Serve sliced with salted butter and some tasty farmhouse Cheddar. Store in an airtight tin.

Dundee cake

Jenny Thomson, formerly of The Butterchurn, Kelty, Scotland. Easily identified by its almond scattered surface, this is a special tea cake often made for festive occasions.

Ingredients

175g (6oz) butter
175g (6oz) caster sugar
4 eggs
rind and juice of 1 lemon
175g (6oz) plain flour
1 teaspoon mixed spice
50g (2oz) ground almonds
100g (4oz) sultanas
100g (4oz) raisins
100g (4oz) currants
50g (2oz) mixed peel
1 tablespoon brandy
25g (1oz) whole blanched
    almonds
1 teaspoon baking powder

1. Line a 18cm (7in) cake tin with greaseproof paper.
2. Preheat the oven to 150°C, 300°F, gas mark 2.
3. Beat the butter and sugar together until pale. Add the eggs 1 at a time, don't worry if the mixture curdles. Add the lemon rind, slowly add the flour, spice and ground almonds to the egg and sugar mix.
4. Once everything is combined, stir in the dried fruit and peel and add enough brandy and lemon juice to make the mixture form a soft consistency.
5. Spoon into the lined cake tin, level the top and bake in the oven for 2½ hours or until cooked. After the first hour of cooking, arrange the blanched almonds around the top of the cake.
6. Cool in the tin before turning out.

Baking

Cornish splits

Traditional, Cornwall. Cornish splits are traditionally served with a Cornish Cream Tea, when they are split and spread with jam and cream. Splits eaten with cream and treacle are known as 'thunder and lightning'.

Ingredients

25g (1oz) yeast
1 teaspoon sugar
300ml (½pt) warm milk
450g (1lb) plain flour
1 teaspoon salt
50g (2oz) butter or lard

1. Add the yeast to the sugar and warm milk and leave to froth.
2. In a large bowl, rub the butter or lard into the flour, add the yeast liquid and mix and knead well.
3. Cover and allow to rise in a warm place until the dough has doubled in size.
4. Knead again and shape into rolls or buns and place on floured baking sheets.
5. Prove again (leave to rise) in a warm place until doubled in size and bake at 190°C, 375°F, gas mark 5 for about 15 minutes.

Barm brack

Traditional, Ireland. This fruit tea bread is found in most Celtic countries. Modern versions are raised by self-raising flour but this is a traditional recipe using fresh yeast.

Ingredients

450g (1lb) strong bread flour
1 teaspoon salt
25g (1oz) butter
5 tablespoons caster sugar
1 egg beaten
pinch cinnamon or mixed spice
225g (8oz) sultanas and currants
    mixed
25g (1oz) mixed peel, chopped
warm honey or sugar dissolved in
    warm milk to glaze

For the starter solution

300ml (10fl oz) warm milk
1 teaspoon caster sugar
25g (1oz) fresh yeast or
    equivalent dried

1. Line the bottom of a 900g (2lb) loaf tin with buttered greaseproof paper.
2. Prepare the starter solution: dissolve one teaspoon of sugar in the milk, and add the yeast. Leave in a warm place for a few minutes.
3. Sieve flour and salt into a bowl. Rub the butter into the flour and add the sugar. Stir in the cinnamon, sultanas, currants and peel.
4. Add the yeast solution and the beaten egg to the flour mixture and work to a stiff dough. Knead well for at least a few minutes. Place dough in the loaf tin. Cover and leave in a warm place for 1 hour to rise.
5. Preheat the oven to 220°C, 425°F, gas mark 7.
6. Remove cover and bake for 5 minutes in the hot oven, then reduce heat to 180°-190°C, 350°-375°F, gas mark 4-5 and continue to bake for another 45 minutes until golden and cooked through.
7. Cool on a rack and brush with warm honey or sugar dissolved in warm milk to glaze.

Bonnag

Michael Smith, from 'A Cook's Tour of Britain', Isle of Man. This is similar to some Irish soda bread recipes and Welsh soda scones. Bonnag is an old Manx word.

Ingredients

450g (1lb) plain flour
1 teaspoon salt
1 teaspoon of bicarbonate of
    soda
1 teaspoon cream of tartar
25g (1oz) lard
300ml (½pt) buttermilk of fresh
    milk soured with 1 teaspoon
    of lemon juice

1. Mix the dry ingredients in a bowl. Rub in the lard until the mixture looks like fine breadcrumbs and add sufficient buttermilk to make a moderately soft dough.
2. Form into rounds, place on greased baking trays and bake at 190°C, 375°F, gas mark 5 for 40 to 45 minutes until risen and golden brown.
3. Cool on a wire rack.

Beremeal bannocks

Catherine Brown, from 'Broths to Bannocks', Scotland. Beremeal bannocks are "earthy tasting bere, pronounced 'bare' (barley) bannocks" from Orkney.

Ingredients

175g (6oz) beremeal or barley
    flour
50g (2oz) plain flour
pinch of salt
1 teaspoon bicarbonate of soda
1 teaspoon cream of tartar
approx. 150ml (¼pt) buttermilk
    (or fresh milk soured with
    lemon juice till it curdles)

Makes 2 very large or 8 small

1. Heat the girdle (griddle).
2. Mix the dry ingredients in a bowl and make a well in the centre. Add the buttermilk and mix with a knife to a soft elastic dough. Divide into two and roll out on a floured board to make two 15cm (6in) rounds.
3. Sprinkle the girdle with beremeal and bake the bannocks on both sides until cooked. Alternatively, small scones can be made by dropping tablespoonfuls of the mixture into a bowl of beremeal, coating and dropping on the floured girdle. Press down lightly and cook on both sides for about 5 minutes.
4. Cool on a wire rack wrapped in a towel. Eat with Orkney butter and farmhouse cheese.

Baking
Welsh cakes

Meudwen Stephens' recipe for Welsh cakes which, with the aid of her mother, she prepares in enormous quantities. Meudwen says the secret of making Welsh cakes is to cook them briskly on both sides so that they stay moist in the middle. Take care not to burn them though! In Wales they are baked on a heavy iron bakestone. Failing this, use a heavy based frying pan or casserole.

Ingredients

225g (8oz) self-raising flour
pinch of salt
1 teaspoon mixed spice
50g (2oz) butter or margarine
50g (2oz) lard
75g (3oz) caster sugar
75g (3oz) currants and sultanas, mixed
1 egg, beaten
1 teaspoon golden syrup

1. Sieve the flour, salt and spice into a mixing bowl. Rub in the fats until the mixture looks like fine breadcrumbs. Add the sugar and dried fruit.
2. Pour in the beaten egg and syrup and stir to make a fairly firm dough.
3. On a floured board, roll or press the dough out to approximately 5mm (¼in) thick. Cut into rounds with a 4cm (1½in) or 5cm (2in) cutter.
4. Bake the Welsh cakes on a medium hot griddle, turning once, until golden brown on both sides but still a little soft in the middle.
5. Dust the Welsh cakes liberally with caster sugar whilst still hot. They are best eaten straight from the griddle, but will keep for up to 10 days in an airtight container.

Treacle and oatmeal biscuits

Ronnie Clydesdale, The Ubiquitous Chip, Glasgow, Scotland. These biscuits have been called Anzac biscuits. As the name suggests, they come from New Zealand, but it seems likely that it was a Scot's hand that put the oatmeal in there. They are particularly good with cinnamon and vanilla ice cream with mango sauce.

Ingredients

100g (4oz) pinhead oatmeal
75g (3oz) plain flour
225g (8oz) caster sugar
75g (3oz) desiccated coconut
25g (1oz) chopped walnuts
100g (4oz) unsalted butter
1 tablespoon golden syrup
1 teaspoon bicarbonate of soda
2 teaspoons water

1. Mix the oatmeal, flour, sugar, coconut and walnuts together.
2. Dissolve the soda in the water. Melt the butter and syrup and the soda and water. Now combine all of the ingredients together and mix well.
3. Place a dessertspoon of the mixture on a buttered oven tray, leaving enough space for it to spread. Repeat with the rest of mixture.
4. Cook in a preheated oven at 180ºC, 350ºF, gas mark 4 for 15 to 20 minutes.

The secret of making Welsh cakes is to cook them briskly on both sides

so that they stay moist in the middle

Baking
Oatcakes

Lynda Kettle, former owner of Ty'n Rhos, Caernarfon, Wales. Welsh oatcakes are similar to Scottish oatcakes but thinner. Both have ancient Celtic origins and are traditionally cooked on a bakestone in Wales. There is a certain art to mixing, rolling or 'rounding', and baking oatcakes. The aim being to achieve an oatcake the size of a dinner plate and as thin as possible. Being a beginner to the art, one can cheat a little. Oatcakes are made infinitely easier to handle by mixing the oatmeal with an equal quantity of wholewheat flour and binding the mixture with a higher proportion of fat.

Ingredients

175g (6oz) medium oatmeal
175g (6oz) wholewheat flour
1 teaspoon salt
¼ teaspoon bicarbonate of soda
75g (3oz) margarine, butter or
    bacon fat
about 2 tablespoons cold water

1. Preheat the oven to 160°C, 325°F, gas mark 3 or oil and heat your bakestone.
2. In a large bowl mix the oatmeal, flour, salt and bicarbonate of soda. Rub in the fat, using your fingertips.
3. Mix to a soft but not sticky dough with the cold water.
4. On a board dusted with wholewheat flour roll out to a large circle about 25cm (10in) in diameter using only half the dough.
5. Either cut the dough into circles using a pastry cutter or leave as one large disc, dividing into 8 portions, like a shortbread.
6. Bake in the pre-set oven for about 20 minutes until pale gold, or griddle, turning once after a few minutes in order to brown both sides.

Abernethey biscuits

Cathleen McLennan, Clifton Coffee House and Craft Centre, Tyndrum, Scotland. This recipe is for a plain biscuit eaten with butter or cheese, from the small village of Abernethey in Perthshire.

Ingredients

225g (8oz) plain flour
½ teaspoon baking powder
75g (3oz) butter
75g (3oz) caster sugar
1 beaten egg
small amount of milk

1. Sift the flour and baking powder into a bowl. Rub in the butter and stir in the sugar.
2. Add the egg and enough milk to make a stiff dough.
3. Turn out onto a floured board and roll out fairly thin. Cut into rounds and prick the middle with a fork.
4. Bake at 190°C, 375°F, gas mark 5 for about 10 to 15 minutes, until golden brown.

Ginger fairings

Cornwall Federation of Women's Institute's 'Cornish Traditional Recipes'. A fairing was a gift brought from a fair by children to parents or by parents to children. It could consist of fruit, biscuits or sweets. The original fairing was two ginger biscuits and two sugared almonds packaged by a Truro lady.

Ingredients

100g (4oz) self raising flour
the grated rind of a lemon
1 level teaspoon of baking powder
1 level teaspoon of ground ginger
1 level teaspoon of mixed spice
1 level teaspoon of ground cinnamon
pinch of bicarbonate of soda
50g (2oz) butter or margarine
50g (2oz) granulated sugar
2 tablespoons golden syrup

1 Mix all the dry ingredients except for the granulated sugar.
2 Rub in the butter, then add the sugar.
3 Heat the syrup until it runs and add to the mixture.
4 Roll in balls the size of a walnut and place on a greased baking tray.
5 Bake on the top shelf of a fairly hot oven, 200°C, 400°F, gas mark 6.
6 When the biscuits begin to colour, remove to a lower shelf where they will sink a bit and develop little cracks.

Carrot and dillisk bread

Gerry Galvin, Drimcong House Restaurant, Moycullen, Co Galway, Ireland. This is a very traditional bread using local dillisk seaweed. It is easiest to buy this in its dried form these days, when it simply needs to be soaked before using. If you can't find dillisk then use any wild seaweed or even some sea vegetables such as sea beet. Don't use too much though because they tend to be salty.

Ingredients

12.5g (½oz) dried dillisk
100g (4oz) melted butter
4 eggs
50g (2oz) caster sugar
1 large carrot, peeled and grated
250g (9oz) flour and a tablespoon extra to flour the tin
1½ tablespoons baking powder

1 Heat the oven to 135°C, 275°F, gas mark 1.
2 Soak the seaweed as instructed on the packet, then finely chop.
3 Grease a 450g (1lb) loaf tin with a little melted butter then flour the tin.
4 Mix together the remaining butter, eggs, sugar, seaweed and carrot. Fold in the flour and baking powder.
5 Pour the mixture into the tin. Bake for 40 to 50 minutes.

Crempog

Melt the butter in the warm buttermilk, then pour gradually into the flour and beat well

Pancakes (crempog)

S. Minwel Tibbott, from 'Welsh Fare', St Fagans: National History Museum, South Wales.
This recipe from Llanfachraeth, Anglesey, where pancakes were an essential part of the welcome given to visitors when invited for afternoon tea in the counties of Caernarvon and Anglesey. They were also prepared there on Shrove Tuesday.

Ingredients

50g (2oz) butter
450ml (15fl oz) warm buttermilk or use fresh milk soured with lemon juice
275g (10oz) plain flour
75g (3oz) sugar
1 teaspoon bicarbonate of soda
½ teaspoon salt
1 tablespoon vinegar
2 eggs, well beaten

1. Melt the butter in the warm buttermilk, then pour gradually into the flour and beat well.
2. Allow this mixture to stand for a few hours, if possible.
3. When ready to bake the pancakes, stir the sugar, the bicarbonate of soda, salt and the vinegar into the beaten eggs.
4. Pour this second mixture into the first one and beat well to make a smooth batter.
5. Drop the batter from a tablespoon on to a well greased and hot bakestone or griddle. Bake over a moderate heat until the pancakes are golden brown on both sides.
6. Spread butter on each pancake whilst hot and serve warm.

(A cupful of sour cream stirred into the batter acts as a further raising agent).

Note: The sudden and unexpected death of Minwel Tibbott in 1998 brought home to her many friends and colleagues just how great had been her contribution to the study not only of Welsh food, for which she was justly well known, but also to the study of women's history in general. Her work in this field was pioneering and survives in the archives of St Fagans: National History Museum, as well as her many publications, as a fitting memorial to a thorough and accessible scholar.

Heavy cake (fuggan)

Traditional, Cornwall. A traditional recipe from a region south of Truro, where seine fishing took place in the fishing village. When the seine net was being hauled in and the men shout "Heave" with every pull, the wives would know the men would soon be in for tea and would make this quick flat cake to be eaten warm or cold. The diamond criss-cross pattern marked on the top with a knife depicts the fishing net.

Ingredients

175g (6oz) plain flour
¼ teaspoon salt
75g (3oz) lard
75g (3oz) currants
40g (1½oz) sugar
a teaspoon of mixed peel (optional)
approx 2 tablespoons of milk

1. Mix the flour, salt and fat roughly together. Add the other ingredients and mix with enough water to make a stiff dough.
2. Roll out to a disc approximately 1cm (½in) thick, and make a patten of criss-cross with a knife.
3. Bake the cake on a greased oven tray at 190°C, 375°F, gas mark 5 for 25 to 30 minutes.

Baking

Marie's brown *Soda bread*

Marie Galvin, Drimcong House, County Galway, Ireland. This is a genuine, old recipe, passed on to Marie from her mother, who had it given to her by her mother. The sprinkling of sunflower seeds is a recent embellishment.

Ingredients

425g (15oz) wholemeal flour
125g (5oz) plain white flour
75g (3oz) butter
2 teaspoons sugar
1 teaspoon salt
1 teaspoon bread soda
300ml (½pt) buttermilk or fresh
milk soured with 1 teaspoon of
    lemon juice
25g (1oz) sunflower seeds
    (optional)

1. Preheat the oven to 200°C, 400°F, gas mark 6.
2. Mix all the dry ingredients together in a large bowl.
3. Rub in the butter until the mixture resembles fine breadcrumbs.
4. Make a well in the centre and add the buttermilk.
5. Shape into a round cake and sprinkle with sunflower seeds.
6. Bake for 35 to 40 minutes.

Marie's brown soda bread

a genuine, old recipe, passed on through generations

Beremeal bread (barley meal)

Colin Craig and Leslie Crosfield, The Albannach, Lochinver, Scotland. Using a little beremeal in this bread gives it a rich, 'earthy' flavour and aroma. Beremeal has been a staple of the North, where wheat was hard to come by, for as long as there has been a population in need of bread! This bread makes a good accompaniment to our game terrine (see starters).

Ingredients

50g (2oz) beremeal flour
½ tablespoon dried yeast
225g (8oz) good organic
    stoneground wholemeal flour
225g (8oz) strong unbleached
    white flour
1 teaspoon of sea salt, finely
    ground
½ tablespoon treacle
a little oil

Makes 2 loaves

1 Dissolve treacle in 150ml (5fl oz) of warm water in a glass measuring jug. Allow to cool until tepid. Whisk in dried yeast, cover with cling film and allow to stand until frothed up to about twice its volume.

2 Meanwhile, mix together the 3 flours and the salt in a large bowl and warm slightly in a low oven. Whisk the treacle and yeast mixture. Make a well in the centre of the flour and pour in the yeast mixture. Mix together by hand adding some more tepid water as required to form a workable dough.

3 Tip out onto a floured work surface and knead by hand for about 10 minutes. Oil a bowl and some clingfilm. Form the dough into a ball and place in the bowl, covered with clingfilm in a warm spot away from drafts for 30 to 40 minutes or until doubled in volume.

4 Knock back the dough and knead for a few minutes. Halve the dough and flatten each half with the heel of your hand to roughly 25.5cm x 25.5cm (10in x 10in).

5 Roll up the dough and squeeze the ends to form two loaves. Place in oiled 900g (2lb) loaf tins. Cover with oiled clingfilm and stand in a warm place for a further 45 minutes or until doubled in volume.

6 Place a bowl of boiling water on the bottom shelf of a preheated oven – 190°C, 375°F, gas mark 5 – then bake the bread for about 25 minutes. Test for readiness by tapping the bottom of the loaf. You should hear a hollow 'drumlike' thud. Return to the oven for a few minutes if it is not ready.

Barley meal

Using a little beremeal in this bread gives it a rich, 'earthy' flavour and aroma.

Planc pastry

Mrs Morfydd Jones, Lochmeyler Farm, Llandeloy, Wales. This large jam tart was a favourite Welsh family treat in the past, and is still prepared in parts of Wales.

Ingredients

225g (8oz) sweet shortcrust
  pastry
100g (4oz) jam
caster sugar to dust

1 Roll out the pastry to 5mm (¼in) thick. Cut into two rounds about 20.3cm (8in) in diameter.
2 Spread one round with jam leaving an edge around pastry. Place the other round on top, making a lid. Moisten the edges with a little cold water and press to seal.

3 Bake the tart slowly on a greased bakestone or griddle, turning carefully during cooking.
4 When golden brown on both sides, and still warm, sprinkle with sugar and serve.

Teisan lap

Babs Meredith, Meredith's Bakery, Llanidloes, Wales. A recipe that was well used in the South Wales mining valleys, this 'moist' cake (for that is the literal translation for lap) served the miners well for their lunch. It didn't crumble or make them too thirsty so it was the ideal filler to pack into their lunch tins and take down the pit.

Ingredients

225g (8oz) plain flour
1 teaspoon baking powder
a pinch of salt
a pinch of grated nutmeg
100g (4oz) Welsh butter
75g (3oz) caster sugar
100g (4oz) sultanas
2 eggs, size 3, well beaten
150ml (5fl oz) buttermilk or fresh
  milk soured with lemon juice

1 Mix the flour, baking powder, salt and nutmeg in a bowl. Rub in the butter then add the sugar, fruit and eggs.
2 Add the buttermilk gradually, beating with a wooden spoon, until you have a mixture soft enough to drop, albeit reluctantly, from the spoon.
3 Bake in a greased and lined 22cm (9in) round sponge tin at

180°C, 350°F, gas mark 4 for 30 to 40 minutes until golden brown and well risen.

Baking
Shortbread

Mary Gilbert, formely of the Coffee Shop at Crinan Hotel, Crinan, Scotland.

Ingredients

225g (8oz) butter
100g (4oz) caster sugar
250g (9oz) plain flour
75g (3oz) cornflour
sugar to sprinkle

Makes 12

1 Cream together the butter and sugar in a bowl. Gradually add the flour and cornflour and mix to form a dough.
2 Either grease or greaseproof line a 30cm x 20cm (11½in x 8in) baking pan. Press the shortbread mixture into the pan and prick with a fork.
3 Bake at 180°C, 350°F, gas mark 4. While still warm, sprinkle with sugar and cut into 12 portions.

Saffron cake

Traditional, Cornwall. The yellow saffron cake is as much a delicacy in Cornwall as the pasty. It is popularly believed that the Phoenicians first brought Saffron to Cornwall when they came to trade for tin. Often made with yeast, this recipe works well using a simple self-raising flour mixture. These amounts make a good sized loaf or shape into small buns if you prefer.

Ingredients

10 strands saffron
1 dessertspoon hot water
6 eggs
350g (12oz) sugar
350g (12oz) butter, softened
350g (12oz) self raising flour

1 Heat the oven to 190°C, 375°F, gas mark 5. Grease and line a 20cm (8in) loose-based cake tin.
2 Infuse the saffron strands in the hot water.
3 Whisk the eggs together, add the saffron water and sugar. Add the softened butter and beat hard to mix, then beat in the flour.
4 Spread the cake mixture in the cake tin and bake for about 50 minutes, until risen and golden. Cool on a wire rack.

Pain d'epices

Traditional, Brittany. This 'bread of spices' from Brittany is the equivalent of Welsh spiced honey loaf, perfect with a strong cup of coffee.

Ingredients

4 level tablespoons runny honey
150ml (5fl oz) boiling water
225g (8oz) plain flour
a pinch of salt
100g (4oz) caster sugar
1 teaspoon mixed spice
1 teaspoon ground ginger
1 level teaspoon bicarbonate of soda
1 level teaspoon baking powder

1. Set the oven to 160°C, 325°F, gas mark 3. Oil and flour a 900g (2lb) loaf tin.
2. Stir the honey into the boiling water.
3. Sieve the flour with the salt and add the sugar and spice. Using a wooden spoon add the melted honey and water, beating until bubbles appear. Stir in the baking powder and bicarbonate of soda.
4. Pour the mixture into the bread tin and bake for an hour or until a skewer inserted into the loaf comes out clean with no trace of dough left on it.
5. Serve the loaf warm or cold, as it is or spread with butter or cream cheese.

Girdle scones, soda scones

Jenny Thomson, formerly of The Butterchurn, Kelty, Scotland. These wedges of floury breads are made with baking soda and without yeast, hence their name – delicious piping hot with butter.

Ingredients

225g (8oz) plain flour
pinch of salt
2 teaspoons cream of tartar
1 teaspoon bicarbonate of soda
50g (2oz) butter
1 egg
5 tablespoons milk

Makes 8

1. Mix the flour, salt, cream of tartar and bicarbonate of soda together in a bowl.
2. Rub in the butter and bind the mixture together with the egg and milk to make a soft but not sticky dough.
3. On a lightly floured surface, pat the dough into a 23cm (9in) circle and cut into 8 triangles, like pieces of cake.
4. Heat a girdle (griddle) and grease lightly with a little oil or lard.
5. Place the scones on it and cook for around 7 minutes on each side.
6. Alternatively cook in a pre heated oven 200°C, 400°F, gas mark 6 for around 10 to 15 minutes.

Drinks and

Home-made drinks reflect a nostalgia for things past. Think of drinks such as traditional ale, mead, cider and mulled wine, which have been around for centuries.

Images of monks and their mead or ale stems from Medieval times, and although most people no longer have time to spend fermenting and preparing their home brew, others living in rural areas cherish such old time beverages. Ginger beer; Cornish samson – or 'egg flip' with cider or mead; Irish carrageen drink and famous Irish coffee; Welsh elderflower cordial and nettle beer; or Scots 'auld man's milk' – an eggnog type drink; and oatmeal drinks are examples of some unusual beverages to try at home.

For those who would also like to try commercially produced Celtic drinks, old fashioned 'scrumpy' and modern cider are still produced in great quantity in Cornwall, and in smaller quantities along the marches in Wales and Brittany where the apple is equally cherished. Traditional ales can be found in good pubs in all the Celtic countries, and whisky is Scotland's great national drink — renowned throughout the world.

As for preserves, a welcome glut of autumn fruits and vegetables means a wonderful array of jams, jellies, pickles and chutneys. The Celts have long gleaned from the countryside to stock up for the colder months. Preserving at home gives great comfort, in the knowledge that there will always be a tasty jar waiting during a barren winter! Unusual preserves like hawthorn chutney, damson jam or rosehip and rowan jellies reveal, yet again, the great forager within the Celt. Likewise, if you have a little time, head for the hedgerows and take out your preserving pan to take pleasure in a real Celtic pastime.

preserves

Elderflower cordial is excellent served with sparkling water, with a drop of gin and a slice of lime.

Put the **damsons** in a preserving pan with half a litre of water. **Bring to the boil and simmer gently until the fruit is soft.**

Bramble jellies

James McWilliams, Dubh Prais Restaurant, Edinburgh, Scotland. Fruit jellies should be bright and clear, not too firmly set. Jellies are best made from fruit rich in pectin and acid.

Ingredients

900g (2lb) brambles
   (blackberries)
300ml (½pt) water
juice of 1 lemon
225g (8oz) sugar for every 300ml
(½pt) of strained juice

Makes around 5 jars

1. Simmer the fruit, water and lemon juice for 1 hour.
2. Strain through a scalded jelly bag, leaving to drip for 1 hour.
3. Add 225g (8oz) of sugar to every 300ml (½pt) of juice.
4. Boil rapidly for 10 minutes until setting point is reached.
5. Take off the heat and remove any scum.

Damson jam

Wendy Brandon, Wendy Brandon's Hand Made Preserves, Boncath, Wales. For all recipes, have ready enough clean and dry screw topped jars, bottle everything while it is still hot, and put the lids on tightly as soon as you fill the jars. For jam and jelly, it is best if you have a proper preserving pan, but if not, make sure that you use a large enough pan that allows the preserve to rise to about 3 times its level when cold. It is by doing this hard, rising boil that you get the jam or jelly to setting point as quickly as possible, thus keeping the flavour and colour. For any preserve with vinegar, do not use a copper or brass pan.

Ingredients

1kg (2lb 3oz) ripe damsons,
   washed and de-stalked
500ml (17fl oz) water
1kg (2lb 3oz) sugar

1. Put the damsons in a preserving pan with 500ml (17fl oz) of water. Bring to the boil and simmer gently until the fruit is soft.
2. Add the sugar and stir until it dissolves, then turn the heat as high as it will go and bring to a rising boil.
3. After 10 to 15 minutes hard boil, take the pan off the heat, stir well and take about half a teaspoon of jam from the centre of the pan and put it on a cold saucer in the fridge. Check after a few minutes and if it forms a skin and wrinkles when you push it with your finger, it has reached setting point and you can bottle it.
4. While the damson jam is cooking, the stones will rise to the top and can be fished out with a spoon if you prefer a stoneless jam.

Drinks and preserves
Atholl brose

Traditional, Scotland. A classic Celtic mixture of oats and water, this used to be served as a beverage once the oats had been drained off, but it can also be a mousse for dessert when the oats are left in.

Ingredients

As a drink

This is the recipe from the late Duke of Atholl
2 tablespoons clear honey
225g (8oz) oatmeal
600ml (1pt) water
Scotch whisky

As a pudding

300ml (½pt) double cream
100g (4oz) lightly toasted oatmeal
100g (4oz) clear heather honey
150ml (5fl oz) Scotch whisky

1 Put the oatmeal in a basin and mix with the cold water to the consistency of a thick paste. Leave for about half an hour then pass through a fine strainer, pressing with the back of a wooden spoon so as to leave the oatmeal as dry as possible. Throw away the oatmeal and use the creamy liquid only.
2 Mix together the runny honey and wineglassfuls of the oatmeal liquid, and stir well. Put into a litre (1¾pt) bottle and fill up with Scotch whisky.
3 Keep for 2 days, and shake well before serving.
4 As a pudding whisk the cream and fold in the other ingredients.

Cornish mead

Traditional, Cornwall. There are similar recipes for mead in other Celtic regions and all have that quaint country feel to them. However, mead is being made commercially again in many regions.

Ingredients

4½l (1 gallon) water
1.2l (2pt) clear honey
2 lemons
4 cloves
25g (1oz) yeast spread on a piece of toast
450g (1lb) white sugar
a sprig of rosemary
a piece of root ginger, about the size of 2 walnuts

1 Boil together the sugar, water and honey, and skim off any scum that might form.
2 Stand in an earthenware basin and add the juice of the lemons and the rind of one. Add the cloves, rosemary and the ginger, well bruised.
3 When this has cooled to blood temperature, or less, add the yeast on a piece of toast (if put into hot liquid, the yeast will be killed).
4 Remove the lemon peel after 3 days, but let the fermentation continue until it has stopped 'hissing', which should be after about a week.
5 Strain and bottle. Cork tightly and leave for at least 2 weeks before drinking. The longer it is left the better.

There are similar recipes for mead in other Celtic regions and all have that quaint country feel to them. However, mead is being made commercially again in many regions.

Rowan jelly

Gerry Galvin, Drimcong House, County Galway, Ireland. The rowan or mountain ash grows widely in Ireland in dry rocky woodlands. It is related to apples and pears and produces bright red berries in late summer into autumn. "A short canoe trip across Lough Aroraun at the back of Drimcong grow the rowan that supply us with berries for this red jelly."

Ingredients

2kg (4lb 6oz) rowan berries
1.4kg (3lb) green cooking apples
   or crab apples
water and sugar

1. Remove the stalks from the berries and wash well.
2. Wash the apples, then core and cut them into quarters.
3. Put both fruits in a large pan and barely cover with water. Bring to the boil and cook for about 20 minutes until soft.
4. Put into a jelly bag or muslin and drip overnight.
5. Measure the juice into a pot and add 450g (1lb) of sugar for every pint of juice.
6. Heat slowly, stirring until the sugar has dissolved and boil rapidly for 8 to 10 minutes until the liquid gels when dripped on a cold plate.
7. Skim and pour into warm, sterilised jars. Cover with waxed circles and seal.
8. Serve with game in winter, or if you have any left with the first spring lamb.

The **rowan** or mountain ash grows widely in Ireland in dry rocky woodlands.

A short canoe trip across Lough Aroraun at the back of Drimcong grow the rowan that supply us with berries for this red jelly.

Auld man's milk

Cathleen McLennan, formerly of Clifton Coffee House and Craft Centre, Tyndrum, Scotland.
This is one of Cathleen's mother's old recipes and it is very much like a Scottish eggnog.

Ingredients

6 eggs
1l (1¾pt) milk
sugar to taste
300ml (½pt) whisky, rum or
  brandy
pinch of nutmeg or grated lemon
  rind

1 Beat the egg yolks, then add the milk and sugar.
2 Add the alcohol then fold in the whisked egg whites.
3 Flavour with nutmeg or grated lemon rind and serve.

Walnut tablet

Mrs McLeod, Tigh-na-Bruaich, Dornie, Scotland.

Ingredients

50g (2oz) chopped walnuts
900g (2lb) granulated sugar
1 tin (400ml) condensed milk
1 cupful (6fl oz) sweet milk

1 Put the sugar, condensed milk and sweet milk into a saucepan and stir until the mixture boils.
2 Boil for 20 minutes then remove from the heat.
3 Add the walnuts and stir until the mixtures thicken. Turn into a greased tin and cut when cold.

Drinks and preserves
Rhubarb and gooseberry jam

Lady Llanover, from 'The First Principles of Good Cookery', Wales. "When boiled, this will make an excellent jam, similar to apricot. It will keep some time in a cool dry place, tied down as usual" (1867). Her original recipe states: "Boil an equal quantity of rhubarb cut up, and gooseberries before they are quite ripe with three quarters of a pound of crystallized moist sugar to one pound of fruit". Below is a modern interpretation.

Ingredients

900g (2lb) rhubarb, cut into 2.5cm (1in) lengths
900g (2lb) unripe or firm gooseberries, topped and tailed
1.4kg (3lb) granulated sugar
juice of 1 lemon

1 Put the rhubarb and gooseberries in a large preserving pan with the sugar and lemon juice. Leave to steep for a couple of hours.
2 Bring to the boil slowly, over gentle heat, stirring all the time until the sugar has dissolved.
3 Boil rapidly until the jam sets lightly or forms a skin when a spoonful is placed on a saucer.

4 Take off the heat and let the jam cool slightly before pouring into warm, clean, dry jam jars. Seal as instructed on the packet of jam-pot covers.

Irish coffee

Eamon Harty, former chef of Mor Chluana Restaurant, Barnabrow Country House, Cloyne, Co. Cork, Ireland. It may feel more like a soporific drug than a coffee, but there's nothing more silky smooth and warming than a well-made Irish coffee. After this, one's only worry is falling asleep!

Ingredients

15ml (½fl oz) Irish whiskey
freshly ground coffee
brown sugar to taste, plus extra for garnish
lightly whipped cream

Serves 1

1 Make the coffee to your own taste.
2 Warm the glass with a rinse of hot water. Pour the measure of whiskey into a long stemmed glass, add the sugar and then the coffee. Pour the coffee until it is a half inch from the rim of the glass. Stir until the sugar is dissolved.

3 Place cream on top of the coffee by heating a spoon and sliding the cream off the spoon, making sure that the cream does not sink into the coffee.
4 Sprinkle the brown sugar on top of the cream for presentation.

It may feel more like a soporific drug than a coffee,

but there's nothing more silky smooth and warming than a well-made Irish coffee.

This is an old
scottish recipe.

For those who like a
dark, slightly bitter taste,
Dundee marmalade is
considered the best.

Marmalade

Theodora Fitzgibbon, 'The Art of British Cooking', recipe from Scotland. For those who like a dark, slightly bitter marmalade, Dundee marmalade is considered the best. The method of making varies from the usual, and is in a way simpler. This is an old Scottish recipe.

Ingredients

1kg (2lb 3oz) Seville or bitter oranges
2 large lemons
2l (3½pt) water
2kg (4lb 6oz) preserving sugar

1. Wash the oranges and lemons and put them into a saucepan.
2. Add the water and put the lid on. Bring to the boil and simmer for about 1½ hours so that you can easily pierce the fruit. When they are ready, take them out and put them on a plate and leave to cool.
3. With a sharp knife slice them neatly and remove any pips. Add these to the juice in the pan. Boil again steadily for 10 minutes and then strain the juice into a preserving pan.
4. Add the sliced, chopped fruit and bring to the boil, then add the sugar. Stir over a low heat until dissolved. Then boil rapidly without stirring to setting point for about 20 to 30 minutes. This makes about 4½kg (10lb).
5. For lemon or grapefruit marmalade the quantities are the same but the fruit should be sliced and chopped beforehand and left to soak in water overnight. The water is used for making the marmalade.

Carrageen drink

Feargal O'Donnell, Wineport Lakeshore Restaurant, Glasson, Co Westmeath, Ireland. "This is a healthy drink that my father used to make for me".

Ingredients

600ml (1pt) water
100g (4oz) carrageen moss
a few fresh lemon slices
a few fresh orange slices
honey to taste
3 cloves

1. Boil the water and add all of the ingredients.
2. Brew to required strength. Strain and serve.

Drinks and preserves
Rosehip jelly

Wendy Brandon, Wendy Brandon's Hand Made Preserves, Boncath, Wales. Rosehips are found in all the hedgerows and are part of country lore. This is a clever use of rosehips devised by the ever canny Celts!

Ingredients

450g (1lb) rosehips, washed and destalked
1kg (2lb 3oz) cooking apples, washed and cut into quarters
400g (14oz) sugar to every 500ml (17fl oz) of juice produced

1 Cover the rosehips with water and simmer gently in a covered pan till soft. Mash them with a wooden spoon.
2 Cover the apples with water and simmer in a covered pan till they are soft. Mix the rosehips and apples together and drip them through a jelly bag. Do not squeeze the bag or you may get cloudy jelly – best to leave it overnight.
3 Then take the pulp in the jelly bag and bring to the boil again, with enough water to cover. Stir well and drip through the jelly bag again.

4 Add both lots of juice together and measure them into a preserving pan. For each 500ml (17fl oz) of juice, add 400g (14oz) sugar – once the juice has come to the boil. Stir well until the sugar dissolves and then bring to a rising boil.
5 After 10 minutes boil, take the pan off the heat and do a setting test (see damson jam recipe).
6 When you are ready to bottle, draw any scum to the side of the pan and ladle out the jelly carefully into the jars, so that there is no scum and no air bubbles.

Nettle beer (diod danadl)

S. Minwel Tibbott, from 'Welsh Fare', St Fagans: National History Museum, Wales.
The drink was regarded as an excellent tonic. This recipe is from Upper Banwy, Montgomeryshire.

Ingredients

225g (8oz) young nettle leaves
100g (4oz) hops
225g (8oz) sugar
1 lemon, sliced
25g (1oz) ginger
25g (1oz) cream of tartar
a little yeast

1 Cover the nettle leaves and hops with water and boil thoroughly.
2 Strain the liquid and leave to cool to blood heat, before adding the remaining ingredients.
3 Finally add a little yeast and allow to ferment overnight.
4 Strain and pour into (sterilised) bottles and cork securely.

Egg flip or sampson

Theodora Fitzgibbon, 'The Art of British Cooking'. This drink is from Cornwall and can also be made with mead. It is similar to a brandy flip and is very good for a cold.

Ingredients

1.2l (2pt) still cider or mead
2 eggs
2 tablespoons sugar

Serves 6

1 Heat the cider, but do not boil.
2 Beat the eggs with the sugar until they are frothy and pour 300ml (½pt) of hot cider over, whisking all the time.
3 Add this to the remaining cider and heat, but on no account boil or it will curdle.

4 Pour into long glasses and serve hot.

Hawthorn berry chutney

Gerry Galvin, Drimcong House Restaurant, Moycullen, Co Galway, Ireland. Hawthorn berries or haws ripen in autumn and fill the hedgerows with colour right into winter. They make a fine chutney.

Ingredients

900g (2lb) haws (hawthorn berries)
600ml (1pt) cider vinegar
1 teaspoon salt
100g (4oz) raisins
325g (12oz) demerara sugar
1 teaspoon each of ground ginger, nutmeg and black pepper
¼ teaspoon each of ground cloves and allspice
juice of 1 lemon

This recipe makes a large batch

1 Snip the haws from their stalks and wash. Put the berries in a saucepan with the vinegar and salt and bring to the boil, cover and simmer for an hour.
2 Rub the contents of the pan through a sieve into a clean saucepan. There should be about 600ml (1pt) of pulp.
3 Add the rest of the ingredients and bring to the boil again. Simmer, stirring constantly, for about 15 minutes until the chutney is thick.
4 Pour into warm, sterilised jars, cover with waxed circles and seal.

Note: This chutney goes well with game and pork. Blended with stock it can be made into a sauce.

Drinks and preserves
Oatmeal drink (stokos)

Cathleen McLennan, formerly of Clifton Coffee House and Craft Centre, Scotland. This is another very traditional Scottish drink. It used to be given to farmers in the hay fields at harvest as it was quite cooling and nourishing.

Ingredients

100g (4oz) oatmeal
½ lemon cut into slices
175g (6oz) sugar
4l (1 gallon) cold water

Makes around 16 glasses or you could halve the recipe to make 8

1 Put the oatmeal, lemon slices and sugar into a large pan and mix with a little warm water.
2 Bring a gallon of water to the boil and pour over the mixture, stirring well.
3 Leave to cool and chill before serving.

Pickled beetroot

Gerry Galvin, Drimcong House Restaurant, Moycullen, Co Galway, Ireland. A lovely old fashioned pickle and very popular.

Ingredients

1kg (2lb 3oz) beetroot, cleaned
   but not skinned
325g (12oz) sugar
1l (1¾pt) white vinegar
150ml (5fl oz) water
3 small, dried red chillies
1 star anise
6 black peppercorns

1 Combine all the ingredients except the beetroot and heat without boiling until the sugar is dissolved. Then bring to the boil and simmer for 2 minutes.
2 In a pot of boiling water, simmer the beetroot for about 1 hour until the skins slip off easily.
3 Pack the beetroot in hot sterilised jars, cover with the hot pickling liquid, cool and seal.

Pack the *beetroot* in hot sterilised jars,

cover with the hot pickling liquid, cool and seal.

Drinks and preserves
Elderflower cordial

Non Henderson, St Andrews Major, Wales. Why not gather some bunches of elderflower from the hedgerows during the early summer when the pretty white blossom smells quite musty? Using this simple recipe you can make enough cordial to last through the winter – and it will keep for a year or two. With its sunny yellow colour and marvellous heady flavour, the strength of the elderflowers gives the cordial a fragrant, almost exotic appeal. Non likes to drink this cordial mixed with some sparkling Welsh water and ice, and agrees that it goes well with a little gin!

Ingredients

65g (2½oz) citric acid
1.75kg (4lb) sugar
1.5l (3pt) water
2 lemons, sliced (optional)
20 heads of elderflower
¼ camden tablet

Makes 1.5 litres (3pints)

1 Put the citric acid and sugar in a saucepan with a little of the water and heat gently to dissolve.
2 Bring the rest of the water to the boil, pour it over the lemons, if used, and elderflowers and add the sugar and citric acid solution.
3 Cover and leave in a cool place for 5 days, stirring well morning and night.

4 Stir in the camden tablet to sterilise the cordial and strain it into clean dry bottles. Store in a cool place.

With its sunny yellow colour and marvellous heady flavour,

the strength of the elderflowers gives the cordial a fragrant, almost exotic appeal.

Cornish punch

Sonia Stevenson, The Old Chapel, Bethany, Cornwall. This very old recipe was used at Levent Mine for many generations, and comes from Lambourne. It would have been for the mine captain's use for his guests and possibly on Accounting day.

Ingredients

1 bottle Jamaican rum
½ bottle Cognac
1 tumbler (1 cup) lemon juice
boiling water
1 whole lemon rind in the piece
900g (2lb) sugar
a dash of Benedictine

1. Put the sugar, lemon juice and rind in a 4½ litre (1 gallon) jug, add the Cognac and rum, and fill up with boiling water poured from a height.
2. Finally, stir in the Benedictine.

Ginger beer

Jenny Thomson formerly of The Butterchurn, Kelty, Scotland. This drink is meant to be made ahead of time, in large batches, and should be stored in glass bottles. It can be kept for up to 6 months in a cool dark place.

Ingredients

6 teaspoons ground ginger
6 teaspoons sugar
2.7l (5pt) water

For the starter

12.5g (½oz) yeast
450ml (¾pt) warm water
2 teaspoons ground ginger
2 teaspoons sugar

To flavour the drink

700g (1½lb) sugar
1l (1¾pt) warm water
juice of 1¾ lemons

Makes around 28 glasses

1. Mix together the starter ingredients in a glass jar with a lid. Stir well, cover and leave on a sunny windowsill for 24 hours.
2. Add 1 teaspoon of ground ginger and 1 teaspoon of sugar daily for the next 6 days. After the 7th day, strain the liquid through a fine sieve.
3. To flavour the resulting drink, dissolve the sugar in the warm water, add the lemon juice and the ginger liquid.
4. Dilute this mixture with the 2.7l (5pt) water, mix well, pour into bottles, cork and leave for 7 days to mature before drinking.

Index

Fresh salmon salt-cured with dill 25
Fried Welsh goats cheese with rhubarb and ginger sauce 28

G

Game soup 47
Game terrine of wild boar, pheasant breast, mountain hare and guinea fowl with a rowan berry sauce 22
Gammon and parsley sauce 104
Garlic:
    Scrambled eggs with cockles and roasted peppers served on a garlic crouton 31
    Roast woodpigeon with pearl barley risotto, chanterelles and wild garlic 124
    Tiny batter cakes of Penclawdd cockles and laverbread on a bed on wilted leaves, with wild garlic mayonnaise or steamed Cleddau mussels 27
Gin:
    Potted hare with Cork dry gin 119
Ginger beer 187
Ginger fairings 161
Girdle scones, soda scones 169
Glamorganshire sausages 75
Goose:
    Michaelmas goose with black pudding and apple stuffing 116
Gooseberries:
    Cornish portland-style mackerel 56
    Gooseberry fool 140
    Rhubarb and gooseberry jam 178
Green cabbage with apple and onion 80
Grouse:
    Whole roast herbed grouse in its own aromatic juices 115
Guinea fowl:
    Game terrine of wild boar, pheasant breast, mountain hare and guinea fowl with a rowan berry sauce 22

Roast guinea fowl with parsnip crisps 121
Guinness:
    Spiced beef 98

H

Haddock:
    Crumbed smoked haddock 61
    Peat Inn smoked fish soup 43
Ham:
    Chicken, ham and leek pie 123
    Cornish chicken pie 114
Hare:
    Game terrine of wild boar, pheasant breast, mountain hare and guinea fowl with a rowan berry sauce 22
Hawthorn berry chutney 183
Heavy cake 163
Herring:
    Manx potted herring 28
Honey:
    Cornish mead 174
    Pain d'epices 169
    Roast leg of Welsh lamb with ginger, honey, cider and rosemary 102
    Welsh honey ice cream 147
Howtowide with drappit eggs 118

I

Irish coffee 178
Irish Mist Liqueur:
    Carrageen soufflé 147
Irish moss ginger jelly 142

K

Kail brose 48
Kale:
    Braised pheasant with curly kale 108
    Colcannon 82
    Kail brose 48
    Seared fillet of wild river salmon with wilted sea kale and oyster cream 64
Katt pie 94
Kerry pies 93

L

Lamb:
    Katt pie 94
    Kerry pies 93
    Lamb, leek and laverbread casserole 100
    Neptune Irish stew 43
    Roast leg of Welsh lamb with ginger, honey, cider and rosemary 102
    Scotch broth with hodgils 41
Laverbread:
    Lamb, leek and laverbread casserole 100
    Laver sauce for roast lamb 102
    Laverbread and bacon pots 25
    Laverbread and oatmeal slices 31
    Laverbread, leek and potato gratin 85
    Salad of Pembrokeshire lobster with a cockle and laverbread dressing 68
    Tiny batter cakes of Penclawdd cockles and laverbread on a bed on wilted leaves, with wild garlic mayonnaise or steamed Cleddau mussels 27
Leek:
    Baked whole black bream stuffed with fresh herbs on tarragon leeks 61
    Caerphilly and leek pancake dome 77
    Chicken, ham and leek pie 123
    Cock-a-leekie 38
    Cream of leek and parsley soup 45
    Lamb, leek and laverbread casserole 100
    Laverbread, leek and potato gratin 85
    Leek and cheese tart 79
Liver:
    Pan fried calves liver and bacon 105
Lobster:
    Salad of Pembrokeshire lobster